CW00924604

DALIA GRINKEVIČIŪTĖ

*TRANSLATED FROM THE
LITHUANIAN BY DELIJA VALIUKENAS*

Peirene

Lietuviai prie Laptevų jūros

AUTHOR

Dalia Grinkevičiūtė (1927–87) was born in Kaunas, the former capital of Lithuania. She spent her teenage years in a Siberian Gulag. At 21 she escaped and returned to her home country only to be deported to Siberia once again in 1951. She was released five years later, then studied medicine. Grinkevičiūtė's writings are now placed firmly in the Lithuanian canon.

TRANSLATOR

Delija Valiukenas was born in Germany to Lithuanian parents, who fled their home in 1944 to escape the Russian occupation. Eventually her family emigrated to the United States and settled in Upstate New York. She earned her PhD in English Literature from Brown University and has taught World Literature for 34 years. Delija writes and translates for Baltic and Lithuanian journals, and was commissioned by the Lithuanian National Theatre of Kaunas to translate several Lithuanian plays into English.

There is only one word to describe this book: extraordinary. It blew me away when I first read it in German translation. Dalia's account goes far beyond a memoir. This is an outstanding piece of literature which should be read by anyone who wishes to understand the Soviet repression.

First published in Great Britain in 2018 by
Peirene Press Ltd
17 Cheverton Road
London N19 3BB
www.peirenepress.com

First published under the original Lithuanian-language title *Lietuviai prie
Laptevų jūros* by Lietuvos rašytojų sąjungos leidykla, Vilnius, 1997
Published under the German-language title *Aber der Himmel – grandios*
Copyright © MSB Matthes & Seitz Berlin Verlagsgesellschaft mbH, Berlin, 2014.
All rights reserved.
This translation © Delija Valiukenas, 2018

With special thanks to Sophie Lewis, who edited *Shadows on the Tundra* for
Peirene.

ISBN 978-1-908670-44-1

The photos in this book have kindly been provided by:

p. 14: Copyright Vytenė Muschick
pp. 9, 10, 21, 40, 70, 85, 202: Copyright Lithuanian National Museum, Vilnius
pp. 137, 149, 168: Copyright Museum of Genocide Victims, Vilnius
p. 128 (top): Aerial view from GRID-Arendal taken by Peter Prokosch
Maps on pp. 6 and 128 (bottom): Copyright Ana Husemann

Designed by Sacha Davison Lunt
Photographic Images (cover): rtsubin/123RF Stock Photo
Typeset by Tetragon, London
Printed and bound by T J International, Padstow, Cornwall

The translation of this book was supported by the Lithuanian Culture Institute.

DALIA GRINKEVIČIŪTĖ

TRANSLATED FROM THE
LITHUANIAN BY DELIJA VALIUKENAS

Peirene

Shadows on the Tundra

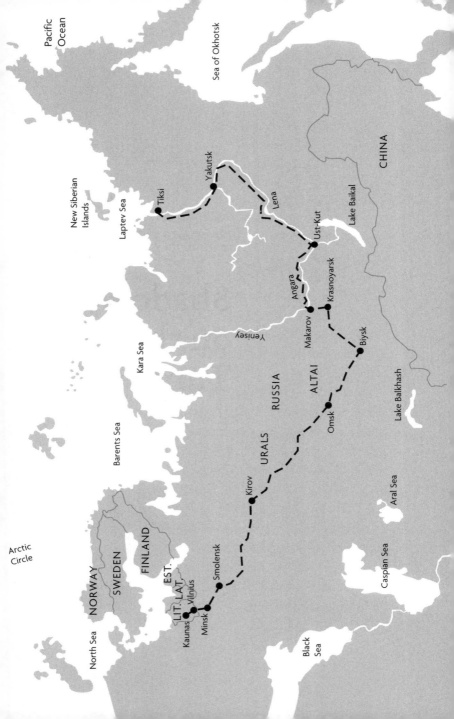

Introduction

On 14 June 1941 Dalia Grinkevičiūtė, a fourteen-year-old Lithuanian girl from Kaunas, was deported along with her mother and brother Juozas. After a journey lasting months and involving many stops, in August 1942 they – together with hundreds of other deportees – arrived on the island of Trofimovsk in the Arctic. Shortly before the onset of winter, they were forced to build a camp for themselves in exile.

Six years later, in 1948, Dalia was given leave to attend college in Yakutsk. Although Dalia's mother was banned from accompanying her daughter, she nonetheless boarded the steamer unnoticed. However, during the journey their deception was discovered. The secret police confiscated Dalia's papers and summarily sent her to the Khangalas coal mine, without letting her say goodbye to her mother. When production stopped at the mine, she was permitted to return to Yakutsk, where her mother was living. Knowing that she was close to death, Dalia's mother wished to see her homeland again and to die in Lithuania.

In February 1949 both women fled illegally, without any papers, to Lithuania from Yakutia via Moscow. When the authorities issued a warrant for their arrest they were obliged to go into hiding with friends and relatives. Fearful of being discovered, the terminally ill mother and her daughter didn't stay anywhere for long.

Such were the circumstances in which Dalia, by then twenty-two years old, under extreme pressure and suffering acute mental strain as a result of living a clandestine existence in hiding, began drafting her memoirs on loose sheets of paper as she moved from place to place. She recalled her initial years of exile as a fourteen- and fifteen-year-old, employing the present tense for her narrative. In the flow of recollections, however, times and places kept changing, often abruptly. Frequently she recounted events as if she were there, but sometimes we see her looking back at the past from her current hiding place. Her happy childhood in Kaunas and her nostalgia for that time are always present too. The memoirs end suddenly in 1942 or 1943.

Throughout the spring of 1950 her mother's condition was desperate, and she died on 5 May 1950. Dalia dug a hole in the concrete floor of the cellar in her parents' house in Perkūno alėja 60 in Kaunas, to give her mother a secret burial. Sensing that she was under observation, she stuffed her sheets of paper into a preserving jar and buried it in the garden. She entrusted her memoirs to the earth, and not a moment too soon, for in late May 1950 she was indeed arrested. Because she refused to cooperate she was sent back to Siberia, via countless prisons and camps in Kaunas, Vilnius, Moscow and Sverdlovsk.

mūsų baratkos tikras
lasonetas. Ginga
vercia vieng po kito.
Ginga sergo ... Ir spiauti
galdma j veido kiekvienam
keris sakys, kad buvo
poliaavijoj i nesirgo c'nga
linga ini kielenenes, tik
skiriasi stadijos. Pas
Piarsioleda two, kad
dauty snegeny bega
krau a. Jie melynii
istry. Paskin
pradedo, klitet ...
Lauky ... brats
... abriar... žoizolos
... nestiancots, skt ir
... kines ... nerestus,
... natine
infekcijos, istet
pirvinkus ... kebiie

prilipusios prie šviežolų,
kurios turbūt uselis
niras bakterijas nuo
šviežolų nuiela. Skanola
sgnarius ir raumepis,
dažniausiai kelius ir
ik klausolas. Viu viskelis
ištikilbeji nes yra ma-
ži an guleti, claugiau
judeti, taikiorioti.
Tš ryto negali atlenkti
kelių jie kaip geli
štiriniai, miš kamui
nuo nauj ir prasukoli
ropoti. Skansota gui an
20 guetio iš štriolu
I klausolas tausi ta
peilių pisaueipe
štiveltkauis deesi
nesoui deip tun
Bet į baraho ko ue

It was not until 1956 that Dalia was permitted to return to Lithuania. She looked for the memoirs she had hidden in her parents' garden, but failed to find them.

In Soviet Lithuania she worked as a doctor in a provincial hospital in Laukuva. The local authorities found the former deportee awkward and in 1974 she was banned from practising as a doctor. Dalia moved in with her close friend Aldona Šulskytė and started writing her memoirs again, this time in a shortened form. That version was disseminated underground and was copied and reproduced many times. By 1979 the memoirs had reached Moscow dissidents and later they made their way to the USA. But they only appeared in a magazine in Lithuania in 1988. Dalia had died of cancer the year before.

Then, in 1991, when Lithuania was free and independent once more, the preserving jar was discovered by chance when a peony was being moved in the garden. The papers were sent to the war museum in Kaunas, where they were conserved and copied. Both versions of Dalia's memoirs appeared in 1997, under the title *Lietuviai prie Laptevų jūros* ('Lithuanians by the Laptev Sea'). Today the original manuscript of her memoirs from 1949–50 is in the National Museum in Vilnius and the text is compulsory reading in Lithuanian schools.

This translation is based on those memoirs written in 1949–50. They reflect Dalia's experiences in exile more directly, emotionally and in greater detail than the later work.

The story of the manuscript mirrors the story of Dalia Grinkevičiūtė. Here sheets of paper have assumed a character of their own – unfaltering, steadfast and strong. Here something so fragile has become an indestructible legacy.

A note in the archive concerning the manuscript reads: 'A total of 229 loose sheets. Recovered from the ground on 22 April 1991 (in Kaunas, Perkūno alėja 60). Written in pencil, ink on plain paper.'

Having had the privilege of meeting Dalia Grinkevičiūtė during the summer holidays at my aunt's house in Laukuva, I made it my mission to ensure that her very personal yet timeless experiences should become accessible in other languages. I am so happy that Meike Ziervogel of Peirene Press has discovered this special book and that English-speaking readers will now be able to read it in this new translation by Delija Valiukenas.

VYTENĖ MUSCHICK
translator of the German edition of
Dalia Grinkevičiūtė's book, *Aber der Himmel – grandios*

Dalia Grinkevičiūtė as a student in Omsk, 1955.

I'm touching something. It feels like cold iron. I'm lying on my back... How beautiful... the sunlight... and the shadow.

I am aware that a phase of my life has come to an end, a line drawn underneath it. Another is beginning, uncertain and ominous. Twenty-four people lie nearby. Asleep? Who knows? Each of them has their own thoughts. Each is leaving behind a life that ended yesterday. Each has a family, relatives, friends. They're all saying goodbye to their loved ones. Suddenly, the train jolts. Something falls from the upper bunk. No one is asleep now. Silence. I dress hurriedly – I have to say goodbye to Kaunas. We are all at the windows. Everything is in the past now, gone for ever. One more jolt and the train lurches forward. I can see the steeples of the Carmelite church gleaming in the sun. It's half past four. Kaunas is asleep. A train with sixty-three covered wagons glides silently into the vast unknown. Fifteen hundred Lithuanians are heading towards an uncertain future. Our eyes fill with tears. The children cry as if they understand – they stare silently at the receding city and the approaching fields. Look, children, have a good look and fix this image, this moment, in your memory for ever. I wonder how many pairs of eyes are taking in their native city for the last time...

'I have a feeling I will never see Kaunas again,' my mother says to me. Her words cut me like a knife. The fight of your life has begun, Dalia. Secondary school, childhood, fun, games, theatre, girlfriends – everything is in the past. You're a grown-up now. You're fourteen. You have a mother to look after, a father to replace. You have just taken your first step in the battle for life.

A tunnel. The train is moving at full speed now. The Nemunas. Petrašiūnai. Where's Dad? Goodbye.

Vilnius. We're at the freight station. Someone is shouting to a relative, a railway worker; he's asking him to tell his mother, to say goodbye, to advise her to pack warm things. To hell with warm things. Advise her to run, to hide. Vilnius recedes. People line the tracks, watching, as though we're being carried off to die. They raise their hands in blessing over us. The Poles are a pious people. Are we really being transported to our deaths?

Hell, no, not on your life. We will not die, we will not give the Devil the satisfaction. And damn the elements. We will live, we will survive. We will fight and we will triumph – hear that?

Naujoji Vilnia. Trains filled with men are lined up at the station. I walk the length of the sealed wagons and enquire about Dad.

No, no, no. The answer is always the same: we're from Vilnius.

We are herded back into our train. The wagons are bolted shut and we begin to move. I had the opportunity to run away back at the station, and I did want to. There were piles of logs nearby, but I remembered that I had a mother who was helpless waiting for me on the train. I was fourteen going on twenty.

'Border, border. We are approaching the border.' The last of Lithuania – the last of her forests, her trees, her flowers.

There's a crack in the door about five centimetres wide. I breathe in the smell of Lithuania's fields. I don't ever want to forget it. Someone starts to sing in one of the wagons – 'How Beautiful Thou Art, Beloved Land of Our Fathers'. Soon the entire train joins in.

Now we are flying across the fields of Belarus. No visa required... Orsha, Minsk, Smolensk. I am thirsty. It is hot and they don't give us much water.

At a station we all slip under the wagons to relieve ourselves. No one feels the least bit embarrassed. When the train next to us pulls out, the view is captivating. In the stations of Belarus we see passenger trains, mostly going to Lithuania. And why not? There will be lots of room soon. Bon voyage to the locusts!

Kirov. We pull in to the station in parade formation: the train from Kaunas is flanked on one side by the train from Riga, on the other by the train from Tallinn. Greetings, Baltic states! Conversations strike up between trains.

Two by two, we queue to collect lunch for our group. Somewhere behind me I see my history teacher. Suddenly – silence. Then a blast from the radio. War! War!

We glance at each other before hurrying back to our wagons with lunch and newspapers.

There is joy on the trains from the three Baltic capitals. Can we be turning round? Going home? But why would we? The front is already behind us. We're also anxious. What is happening in Lithuania? Is there much devastation? Have any relatives been killed during the bombing? Our journey goes on. And on and on. Day five, day ten. We don't eat everything we have; we give some bread to the local children with their outstretched hands and ravenous eyes, pleading in Russian, '*Khleba, tyotenki…*' – 'Bread, aunties…' It was a refrain we started to hear as soon as we crossed the border and left Lithuania.

The Urals. Greetings, Mother Asia… Tired, dirty, pale, we sleep on top of each other. We have only one question and are interested in only one topic of conversation: where are they taking us? We had thought the Urals, but we've already passed them. Andriukaitis, formerly a merchant, and a practical man, is drying his ration of bread and trying to convince the rest of us that we'll be buying it from him soon. A salesman by nature, he plies his trade even here: buying, selling, swindling. 'You'll be living in mud huts and lynching each other,' he says, as he chews, his mouth full. As if that possibility applied only to us and not to him too.

Every serving of millet porridge that we get, he's the only one to eat it. He says, 'So don't eat it, see if I care. You'll regret it soon enough.' There are whole buckets of the stuff. We pour it down the hole onto the tracks. But the wheeler-dealer Andriukaitis had spoken the truth, for we often remembered that porridge, and not that long afterwards either.

Day fifteen, day twenty. My head feels heavy, I am weak. Finally! We reach the finishing line. At each station, between three and five wagons are uncoupled. Western Siberia. Troschin Station. The doors to the covered wagons are slid open. '*Vygruzhaytes bystreye!*' – 'Out! At the double!' No matter how often I hear the expression in later years – variously embellished with Russian swear words – my blood freezes. Where are we? What fate awaits us?

We are in a public square sitting next to our belongings and being sorted by destination. Stalin's 'disciples' sidle up to the clusters of deportees and rummage through their possessions. It is pouring. Claps of thunder. Mothers cover their children, but everyone gets soaked.

Four hours later, the process comes to an end. An announcement is made: '*Tak vot, vy budete zhit v sveklo-sovkhoze.*' – 'Right, you people will be living on a collective beetroot farm.'

The nineteenth and twentieth wagons (with fifty deportees in all) are bound for the collective farm. Whenever roll call was taken on the train I found it unsettling to be addressed by number. I feel the same discomfort now when the Chekist, a guard from the secret police, shouts, 'Number seventeen!' Number seventeen? It takes several minutes to register, then I feel the blood rush to my face, my heart pound. Number seventeen from wagon nineteen – that is who I am! I'm glad Dad isn't with us to hear it.

It's like being in chains. Each of us is called in turn. The swarthy Chekist with the steely eyes gives me a look that feels worse than a blow. It is the look of a slave merchant, assessing my muscles, calculating the amount of work that he can squeeze out of me. For the first time in my life, I feel like an object. No one seems to care that I'm not in school, studying as I should be. I stand, haggard and ashen. I harbour the slave's terrible hatred and resentment. Turning my head, I notice Mother. She is standing a short distance away, watching me with an expression of pain. She is the first to react and immediately lowers her eyes, but I can see the tears on her cheeks. Her daughter and her son, their parents' pride and joy, being sized up like work animals. We understood each other. It was an uncomfortable moment for both of us and we've never talked about it since.

We are housed in two huge barracks and work eighteen hours a day in the fields. No one complains, though it is hard at first. Our faces grow sunburned, our hands rough and calloused. We are paid almost nothing. Our supervisors never pass up an opportunity to taunt us; in their view, we're criminals. The Ukrainians, who are also deportees, are warm-hearted. We don't speak a word of Russian but somehow muddle through. We feed ourselves by bartering. Winter arrives. The barracks are as cold as outhouses. People move – some are resettled in Troitsky, others in Biysk, and the Ukrainians are resettled with other Ukrainians.

We all believe that we'll be going home soon. No one thinks otherwise. The climate here is good, especially for

Left: Dalia's mother Pranė Grinkevičienė (1898–1950) in Kaunas.
Right: Dalia's father Juozas Grinkevičius (1892–1943) in a camp in the northern Urals.

people with tuberculosis. My friend Irena B., who's my age, was being treated for a collapsed lung in Lithuania, but here she has filled out like a sweet bun. The winter is cold but dry. It doesn't linger. Spring is on the way and we will be planting vegetable gardens soon.

If only I could sleep – if only for a minute, even a second. The train rocks from side to side as it speeds along at full throttle, howling dully. The seventy-two people in our wagon are sleeping on their feet with their eyes open. I can feel someone breathing beside me and shivering. It's Genė Markauskaitė, the tubercular ten-year-old girl with skin the colour of lemons, sunken eyes, blue lips. She has the chills, while I'm roasting. Lice crawl solemnly across her neck and shoulders, then cross over to me and disappear.

Krasnoyarsk. This hellish train journey has now lasted a week. In the darkness, a small light flickers from the ceiling of our wagon. Is it possible that I once used to sleep at night? That I was able to stretch out my legs? No, it's beyond belief.

There's no room to move – my legs have swollen up. A haze has settled over everyone in the wagon. I see Genė's face as though in a dream. She's coughing at me. Why in hell have we had to breathe in each other's face and fatten each other's lice for the last five days?

Now they're brawling, the vipers. Some fat idiot is hitting Genė's mother with a stick for leaning against him. Bastards, scumbags, they'll be dead soon enough, yet they're at each other's throats. If only there were fewer people – even one or two fewer – there'd be more room to breathe. Screams. Hysteria. Any minute now, I'm going to die of suffocation. I dream without sleeping. The journey is inhumanly long. I find myself wishing that the train would fly off its tracks, that the wagons would smash open – anything, just to be able to breathe. I must be going mad.

Finally. We arrive. The wagon is emptied. Solid ground. Legs that haven't walked in a week buckle. Rain. Mud. The barracks are 500 metres away. We drag our belongings. It's a huge place, filthy and packed with unwashed bodies steaming where they lie on the floor and reeking of their rags. Ten or so minutes later, five thousand people are asleep in the stable, or perhaps it's a club hall. How good it feels to stretch out and let my legs relax at last. Silence.

We learn that we are in Makarov, near the Angara River. A brisk and energetic young man by the name of Zienčikas guesses that we'll soon be boarding a steamer. Everyone's eyes light up. We are all swept along in the excitement of thinking that we're bound for that utopia called America. Some don't believe it but most want to. Even if Zienčikas turns out to be wrong, we will have lived in hope for two weeks, buoyed up by the illusion of a quick liberation. Numerous occasions come to mind which seem to corroborate the general belief. Zigmas Steponavičius, who'd been a student at the Academy of Agriculture, had sold his watch to a guard, then the watch stopped. The guard was furious: 'How's that for ingratitude. Here we are transporting these Lithuanians to good places and this is how they repay us.' But I'm not convinced, because if there had been a directive to transfer Lithuanians to America, they'd have transferred everyone. So why was Matiukenė, whom the farm supervisors really liked, left behind? But even I give in to the general enthusiasm. We're off to America or to the American territories, as Krikštanis would have us believe. I think of him as an authority figure. This is a time when I defer to everyone in authority and have no opinions of my own.

We are on our way to the steam baths. In order to have more time for washing, we try to get there first, right after the announcement is made. I think 'we' were me, the Morkus girl and, I'm guessing, Zienčikas's daughter. The bath is huge. Apparently built to wash the groups heading north and east. A handsome young man collects our clothes. He asks us who we are. We tell him we're Lithuanians. He tells us that the Finns, Estonians and Ukrainians have already come through. He urges us to undress quickly before the place fills up with women. The three of us look at each other in astonishment. We ask why a woman isn't working here. 'The woman is in the men's section,' he replies with a grin. Well, there's nothing to be done about it. We undress and hand him our clothes, which he hangs on hooks to be deloused. The bath leaves us feeling cleansed and refreshed. 'Pretty Boy' greets us pleasantly and hands back our clothes. We dress calmly and, in all sincerity, wish him a cordial goodbye. That same evening we are transferred the few kilometres by truck to the shores of the Angara River. We are housed in several large wooden sheds. Those of us who cannot fit in remain outside. We spend a week there. I even manage to take the train to Cheremkhovo to sell a few things. I return with flour, butter and other food.

The evenings here were extraordinary. Bonfires were lit after sundown. We were living in a forest, so branches were plentiful, and we kept the fires going till dawn. Everyone would gather around the bonfires – young and old alike. In that great expanse, the fires glimmered like so many specks of light and Lithuanians by the thousand sang to forget their troubles. The forest trembled with their mighty sound. We usually began with the deportee anthem, 'Return Us to Our Fatherland'. I am neither musical nor sentimental, but this song would shake me to my core, every time. I can't imagine any choir, any music, any melody anywhere sounding more beautiful than the songs the Lithuanian deportees sang on the forested shores of the Angara River. The singing would begin at one bonfire and be picked up at another, then at a third, and so on and on, until the immense forest filled with the anguished Lithuanian melodies. We would find ourselves back in the Lithuania of our dreams, and we would weep. The songs united us, they gave us strength, warned us of the hardships ahead, and inspired the sons and daughters of Lithuania to endure. For one brief moment, the songs drew us closer to our homeland, encouraged us not to lose hope of returning. I don't know how the others felt, but whenever I looked at the deportees gathered in song, I couldn't help wondering how many of them would ever see their homeland again. I'd get a bad feeling, as though I was seeing the shadow of death hovering above some heads. Perhaps it was only a child's intuition. Yet time would confirm it. Oddly, I never thought that I might die. I believed absolutely that no matter what the future had in store, I would survive. It was as simple as that. During the days that followed, a kind of tenacity began to take shape as part of my character. I became stubborn. I felt a growing desire to confront life, to grapple with it, to prevail. I was convinced of my survival.

We are being moved into boats – barges, actually. For two days we float down the swift Angara River. The days are sunny, the shoreline picturesque. I don't feel like thinking, my head is empty. Again we are made to disembark, again it rains. Why does it always rain when we have to disembark? The shore is rocky. In a few hours it becomes a settlement. The steamer with its convoy of barges reverses course. It is heading back to pick up the rest of our party, as well as the deportees who have still to arrive in Makarov. Dusk. Tiny campfires flicker here and there. We boil up gruel just to fill our stomachs. The forest is some distance away. There is no firewood, nothing but empty space – as far as the eye can see – seeded with rocks and Lithuanian 'gypsies'. We assemble our bedding out of rags pulled from our sacks. Everything is either damp or soaking wet. It is cold and unpleasant. But the air is clean. Our little colony settles down for the night. We lie next to each other and spread everything we own over ourselves. I breathe under the covers where it is warm, despite the rain. Water gathers in the folds of the covers and seeps, drop by drop, onto my knees. An east Siberian rain washes my hair.

It's a cloudless, cold night. Five hundred Lithuanians on a rocky beach in Zayarsk.

'Didn't I tell you? It's perfectly clear, clear as day, my dear Broniuk. We were not mistaken – we are heading for the American territories,' Krikštanis says to his wife, after catching his breath. He has noticed that people are being loaded onto lorries and driven along the shore to the wharf on the Lena River. Krikštanis is our group elder. Even though we're not on the train any more, we've come to constitute a body of people who have been travelling together in covered wagons since the start of our deportation. Each such party of deportees is now fed and transported as a unit. Krikštanis is the black sheep. He left Lithuania voluntarily. On 23 June, when the Germans were bombing Vilnius, he retreated into the interior of the Soviet Union with his wife and son. Afraid of being mobilized by the Germans, he withdrew even further: Gorky, Moscow, Saratov, Tashkent, Barnaul. When he heard that Lithuanians were being deported, he joined our convoy, which he assumed was bound for the American territories.

'I'm a democrat,' he explains, adjusting his pince-nez with two fingers. 'I fought and will continue to fight for the interests of the majority – that is my motto.'

He'd spent three years in a Kaunas prison. Generally speaking, there is little to like about him, but he's good to his family. I remember one occasion, back in Biysk, when we were being loaded onto wagons, everyone pushing and shoving to get in – you'd think we were afraid of being left behind. As a result, we sat like sardines, cheek by jowl. I remember Krikštanis hoisting himself up by the handles on the side of the red wagon, using his body and feet to push everyone else aside in order to be first on the train. I stood apart and watched, thinking, here's someone who'd climb over corpses if they got in his way.

Lorries appear at ten- to fifteen-minute intervals. Twenty adults with their children and belongings climb aboard and disappear in a cloud of dust. The day is hot. No shade whatsoever. Everything that had been wet or damp has dried. By evening, only a quarter of the deportees remain. The loading area on the beach is nearly empty. It starts to get chilly. Then cold. I put on my winter coat. Several bonfires remain lit across the enormous space, abandoned by the deportees who didn't get a chance to cook anything before the lorries arrived. Construction boards that had been swiped from somewhere have nearly burned through. A girl my age is sitting at one of the fires. I approach and pause on the opposite side of the blaze. Like myself, the girl is wearing her scout uniform. I notice how animated she is. I notice her blue eyes and blonde plaits. The classic Lithuanian girl, I think to myself.

'I saw you in the barracks at Makarov. Are you from Kaunas?'

'Yes, I am. And you?'

'I'm from Šiauliai.'

We examine each other, but find nothing more to say. I walk away as a lorry pulls up and my new acquaintance climbs in. The lorry speeds off. So much for making friends. Would we ever meet again? I wonder. But life will bring us together, and in intriguing circumstances.

At half past four the following morning, at first light, a lorry pulls up to our group and we shove our way in. Not everybody from our train group makes it. Only about twenty-five of us. I remember Krikštanis, Noreikienė with her son Dalius, Nausėdienė, Jasinskienė with her daughter Dalia, Albertas Janonis with his mother, Dovydaitienė with her daughter Birutė, Žukienė and Grockis, among others. Within minutes we're off, speeding down a paved road to join the convoy of lorries that left earlier. The day, 25 July, is going to be hot and we will cover a lot of ground. It's around 300 kilometres from the Angara River to the Lena. The drivers are experienced and go at top speed. On the turns, the lorry tilts and we scream. I ask the driver to slow down to ninety kilometres an hour, at most. He climbs out of the cab, steps onto the running board, lets go of the wheel while we're still moving fast, and looks at us. At the sight of our terrified faces, though, he stops fooling around. We drive through forests inhabited only by wildlife. Not a living soul for 300 kilometres in any direction. Giant trees lie untouched where they fell at the beginning of time. Forests and more forests – mighty, impassable, primeval. Forests into which no man has ever set foot. To think that the Soviet Union has run out of paper. Far away in Stalingrad, all stands ready for a great battle. Armies gather, warplanes roar and artillery booms. Here all is quiet, just the sound of Lithuanian deportees being carted to the wide Lena River. There is no water and I'm thirsty. Face, eyes, mouth – our bodies have been sealed by dust. Albertas and I settle on top of our belongings at the back of the lorry to feel the breeze.

Suddenly, Jasinskienė lets out a savage scream, her eyes bulge, she throws aside her two-year-old daughter Dalia, and tries to strangle herself. The men tear at her hands, but she clutches her neck hysterically. The blue veins on her forehead bulge. The men succeed. We find some water, dab her face, give her a drink. The woman returns to normal. Again she presses her darling girl to her breast, again she kisses her, eager to live. Oh, those nerves of ours... they are so hard to control, especially for a deportee.

Around three o'clock in the afternoon, we stop and head for the woods. A red carpet as far as the eye can see: berries. They refresh us somewhat, we are less thirsty. After a break of several hours, we're off again. Downhill all the way. The crazy driver does not slow down, but each kilometre brings us closer to the Lena River. Day turns into evening. Then night. It gets cold. The lorry drones on without stopping. I feel uneasy. Albertas and I stare into the pitch-black darkness on either side of the road. Nothing but forest: gloomy, desolate, impenetrable. I enjoy sitting at the back of the lorry next to him, as we hurtle into the darkness of this uncharted and endless forest. Albertas. The young man with the beautiful soul. He was a drama student in Šiauliai, but I think he must have graduated from the university by now. He loves nature and people. He's a kind and gentle soul. For some reason, he reminds me of Alyosha in Dostoyevsky's *The Insulted and Injured*. A tall, slender, blond, handsome and blue-eyed lad. 'The theatre, Dalia, is my dream, my life's goal, my alpha and omega. As soon as the war is over, I'm returning to the stage. I want to elevate people's lives, to awaken their noblest feelings. Life, after all, is so beautiful, so wonderful, so exciting,' Albertas would often say to me, while his blue eyes flashed and smiled. I begin to droop. We draw closer to Ust-Kut, the wharf on the Lena River. It's half past six in the morning. It has taken us exactly twenty-four hours to get here. Our lorry pulls into a tent city. We slip into the first available tent and fall asleep.

We spend two weeks here waiting for a steamer. The *Moskva* and the *Lermontov* have already made two round trips. The 'American territories' theory appears to be holding. Sceptics are called pessimists, blockheads, killjoys and whiners. People obviously want to believe their guide and mentor. Such optimism should not be discouraged. The days are beautiful, we take steam baths and are fed well. Half a kilo of bread per person and barley porridge three times a day. It's like a spa resort. Our immediate neighbours in the tent are the family of Professor Vilkaitis. I'm rude to him. During the day, when everyone is out picking berries, I stay behind. The professor asks why I don't join the others.

'I don't care for berrying,' I say.

'But you'd get a chance to see many beautiful and interesting plants that are native to this region,' the professor insists, eyeing me with a smile.

'Oh, botany, I hate botany. I have to confess, I really have no interest in it,' I babble pompously. Then I remember that Vilkaitis is a botanist and bite my tongue. He smiles forgivingly.

'I spent eight years in school with your dad. We shared the same desk and he was a good friend. Who knows, perhaps some day we'll meet again.'

'Perhaps...'

On the other side of the tent are the Balčius family from Daugai, in Dzūkija. They're very nice people. He is a former teacher and squadron commander with the Riflemen's Union. I'm surprised that he wasn't separated from his family and deported to a labour camp. In the evening, there are songs – sad, beautiful songs, filled with homesickness and longing. A child is crying. Four days ago, his mother got lost while picking berries and never returned.

We're on the shores of the Lena. Waves pound in. The river is wide. The steamer *Nadezhda Krupskaya* stands at the dock with two large barges in tow. We are moving into one of them. Our 'disciples' are in charge. Because they are passenger barges, they're reasonably comfortable. Each of us has a berth of sorts, and we have not been separated from our train-mates, which makes us happy. We've become used to each other; we're almost friends. Again we spend the night on the rocky shore, listening to the crashing waves. I stand at the water's edge and stare at the Lena, wondering how many men and women the Tsar deported downriver to remote places of exile. How many young, gifted sons and daughters have been transported by these very same waves, never to return? How many perished in exile? How many hopes and dreams vanished along the way? Banishment crushed their youthful spirits, dampened their enthusiasm, blunted their feelings and consumed the best years of their lives. And where are they taking us? Can it really be to America? I know in my bones that I should stop fooling myself. I still have a long battle ahead. Your fight for life is not going to be easy, Dalia. In the dark of the night, the river turns black. Waves continue to pound the shore and a light mist is falling.

The landscape glides slowly past our barge: farms and fields, herds of cattle, sand dunes. Gaggles of children play on the beaches, they swim, they call to us and wave. The sunny days drift along one after the other. The *Nadezhda Krupskaya* tows our barges towards the mouth of the Lena. Everyone is upbeat. We are fed three times a day and given as much water as we can drink. We bathe frequently and can wash our clothes; we look more youthful, livelier. For the young, it is like a field trip. A school holiday. They wear their best clothes, mostly the ones they brought from Lithuania.

Indeed, the young look radiant. It does feel like an excursion on the Nemunas, people setting out on a day trip. Here and there, couples can be seen chatting and flirting. The sounds of an accordion and singing can be heard from the barge up ahead. A few days later, we dock in Kirensk, which is on the border with Yakutia. Onions, milk and dried fish are sold at the dock for cash. It seems that money has value here.

We sail on. A skiff from one of the barges heads to shore to bury someone who has just died. It is midday and completely quiet. Peaceful. Our entire journey is like this. It lasts a month. We stop only for burials on one of the Lena's many islands or beaches. Fresh wooden crosses are a frequent sight along the river. I make a point of always turning to watch the grave of the unknown deportee vanish into the sunlit horizon. You poor unfortunates, never again to set eyes upon the sunny shores of the Nemunas or the Dubysa. The wind that blows across the fields of Lithuania will never sweep across your graves. Once the war is over – if we survive – we may one day go home, but you never will. The occasional barge or steamer will glide by. Maybe a passenger or two will cast a glance at your solitary grave. But no one will ever come to tend it or plant a flower. Even the inscription will eventually weather away – not that there would be anyone in this desolate place to read it. What an irony! To think that a person has lived, studied and worked only in order to end up here. If someone had told a deportee, while they were still living in Lithuania, that this was to be their final resting place, they wouldn't have believed it. We are all optimists, after all. I'm also one of those who imagine themselves immune to death and prison, when in fact I could be shoved underground like a dog myself…

Oh, sunlit days! How often we remembered this time when life became difficult – it was our holiday escape, our journey on the Lena. Songs in the evening. The most energetic people here come from Marijampolė. Their young are especially patriotic. I have no girlfriends, so I spend most of my time with the adults.

Žukienė fancies herself a lady and rustles about the open deck of the barge in a long red silk kimono. Even during our deportation's most perilous moments, she kept her nails manicured and gave herself facial massages to keep her skin clear. Because she was a colonel's wife, she feels superior to the rest of us, though she has become the target of jokes, poor thing. There were two Jews, a brother and sister, I can't remember their surnames, just the sister's name – Dora. They owned a windmill in Šiauliai. Žukienė demanded their assistance, promising to intercede with her husband on their behalf, should they decide to rebuild their windmill after the war. When we were living in the Altai territory, she even buttonholed Adolis Ašmantas, a sickly fifteen-year-old, asking him to gather some firewood for her from the forest in return for preferential admission to the military academy. The practice of bribery had become so deeply ingrained in her that even in exile on another continent she was still trying to work the system. Her husband was almost certainly not deported, or so I believe. He stayed behind in Lithuania, probably went into hiding.

Krikštanis, the born orator, can't seem to live without an audience. Whenever he finds someone who will listen to

35

him, he predicts that the Soviet Union will lose the war. I don't understand why he wanted to leave in the first place.

We enter the forest region. The river narrows, its banks are high and steep. As we are heading due north, the area is fascinating from a geographical point of view. I get to see every possible zone: deciduous, evergreen, taiga, tundra, and all the things in between. The changes in vegetation are clear to see.

Yakutsk. We are told to disembark with all our belongings because the barge is going to be disinfected. We are hustled to the steam baths. The sick are instructed to remain, to be taken to hospitals in town. Mother is ill, and we could have remained with her in the city, but the three of us do not want to be separated from our train-mates, so we say nothing. Late at night, we are moved back into the barge, which is anchored mid-river. A double-decker boat, the *Pyatiletka*, passes by. There's light in the windows, we hear music, a cool breeze ruffles my hair. I inhale the splendid sight of that wondrous boat and dream of living well. To think that there are people who are free to travel on a steamer like that, that somewhere life is free and beautiful. I feel myself getting stronger, more determined; my desire to live, to fight, to endure intensifies. I want to take life by the horns, I want to take charge of it rather than have it knock me about. We've got a life to live yet, Dalia, and a battle to fight. Life may be a cruel enemy, but we will not surrender. So what if I'm only fifteen.

*

Another week, then ten days slip by. The trip by barge has not been boring. I am lying in my berth, pretending to be asleep. I want to watch Štarienė flirt with a soldier. She's a very pious lady, or so she would have us believe. A real patriot. Whenever she hears a child singing a Russian song, she smiles sarcastically and scolds the parents. Meanwhile, she herself is making out with Chekists and Russians. My brother Juozas has nicknamed her 'Sweet Genutė'. She *is* pretty, but thoroughly devious. She'll smile at a Russian and, next thing you know, he's flipped her on her back and is groping her. When she talks about her husband, who's in the labour camps, those blue eyes seem to shed real tears. A regular Jesuit, that one. Her best friend, Stasė Prapuolenienė, with whom she has thrown in her lot, is in love with Genutė and doesn't notice how two-faced she really is.

A rumour has been making the rounds regarding the Lithuanians who were transported earlier to seagoing ships in Tiksi, an Arctic Ocean harbour, and then taken… where? 'To America, of course,' say the 'Americans'. Some of the rumours are very specific, like the one about people tossing their work clothes into the sea because they won't be needing them in America. This was, supposedly, reported by a sailor from Tiksi. What is going on here?

Only later, after I'd swallowed the 'American theory' whole and left for Tiksi myself to attend school, did I finally understand. There had been some truth to the rumours, but those seagoing ships transported our countrymen only to the mouth of the Yana River, where they died, just like us on the Lena. And yes, people did toss things out, because they thought that they were heading for America. The barometer of hope always went up after rumours like these.

Meanwhile, Bulun is getting closer. The further north we sail, the harsher the climate becomes. Sunny days cease altogether; storm and wind are now constants on the river. The forests thin and the trees shrink. In Bulun, the regional centre, we experience our first serious shock: half of us are told to disembark. What about America? The rest sail on. To Tit-Ary – and a fish-processing factory. Several hundred more people are unloaded. Genė Morkutė – one of the most determined 'Americans', a kleptomaniac, light-fingered girl – refuses to concede defeat. As she disembarks, she shouts back at us, 'Not to worry, we're just going to the baths, and then – then it's straight for the American steamships. Those are the facts.' Oh, those facts, how tiresome they have become. In Tit-Ary, several hundred people wait on the shore with their belongings, presumably to be taken to the baths. Unfortunately, these 'baths' would be the death of many for whom the 'American steamships' never arrived.

We pull away from Tit-Ary. What now? The trees disappear. All vegetation disappears. The larches shrink to forty or fifty centimetres and then vanish altogether. We have arrived in the land of tundra. We see a bear, which placidly turns to look at our convoy without interest.

The rock of Stolby, some 100 metres high, rising clear out of the water. More people are unloaded at the island. I watch Lithuanian families clamber onto dry land. A keen wind blows sand into their mouths and noses. The river is rough, rope ladders toss in the wind. And the whole of Stolby island – just two tents.

We pull away, leaving a hundred countrymen behind on the 'American' shore, sitting on their bundles with their children. Being assailed by a sandstorm. Several hours later, another stop.

The riverbank is steep. A barge carrying bricks has docked along the front. I see people unloading the bricks and carrying them ashore on their backs. Several tents and two small, unfinished wooden structures – without windows, roof or floor – stand on the summit. It is 28 August 1942. I watch more barges being manoeuvred towards the shore. So this is 'America', I think. A bitter wind is blowing in from the mouth of the Lena and the river is white with foam. Not a hint of vegetation anywhere. A cold, bleak and barren coast. This has been our destination all along. One of the 'disciples' shows up and orders our barge to be loosed. '*Nu vot, priyekhali*,' – 'Well, here we are' – he says, smiling. Then, with obvious irony, he asks, '*Chto, ne nravitsa?*' – 'What, don't you like it?' A cheap shot. How cynical do you have to be to make fun of women and children whom you've brought to the mouth of the Lena River and left for the winter?

We are on the shore, or rather at the foot of the riverbank. We drag our things up the high, crumbling slope. The sand pulls us backwards, we slip and fall with our belongings. No one feels like talking, we are all depressed. Four hundred and fifty Lithuanians are standing on polar tundra, looking for the city.

Dalia with her brother Juozas
wearing school uniform, early 1930s.

'Where will we live?' we enquire of a well-dressed man walking by with the look of someone in charge.

'You'll be building the place yourself,' he replies with a smile. 'You're in luck. Several tents have already been set up. When we arrived two weeks ago on the convoy of barges, we found nothing but bare earth. Just a sign left by a previous expedition that read: "This is the site of a future *rybzavod* – a fish-processing factory – and the name of the place is Trofimovsk."'

The man is clearly proud of himself. Look at us, he seems to be saying, we've conquered the North Pole; we're building cities on the tundra.

I look around and am chilled to the bone. Far and wide, tundra and more tundra, naked tundra, not a sprig of vegetation, just moss as far as the eye can see. In the distance, I notice something that looks like a small hill of crosses. We learn that these are the graves of the Finns. Two weeks ago, they were brought in from Leningrad already debilitated as a result of the blockade, starved and suffering from typhus, and now they are dying. Suddenly, I'm gripped by fear. What if this becomes a 'death *zavod*' rather than a 'fish *zavod*'? I hear the steamer sound her horn and start to move, manoeuvring our empty barges through a maze of rafts.

Oh, horror. I want to grab hold of a barge and scream, 'Wait, don't leave us! Where have you brought us?' But the line of barges recedes, leaving us behind on this uninhabited island of Trofimovsk, where the polar winter that lasts ten months of the year is about to begin.

But live we must. As we stand here in the empty field, the dandy we met earlier is back and orders us to start piling bricks. We learn that his name is Sventicki and he is the foreman in charge of the construction of the future *rybzavod*.

'Where do we sleep?' we ask him.

'The sooner you start stacking the bricks, the sooner you'll have a place to live. Bricks – everyone!' he shouts, and runs off.

Some stack bricks, others stack boards and various other building materials. I go below deck to get some rope to tie the bricks together. I notice that the men, including Stankevičius and Krikštanis, carry twelve to fifteen bricks at a time, but I can't manage more than seven. The work goes something like this: three metres up a steep ladder from the cargo hold, then across the deck to a gangplank and down the gangplank to the shore. Overall gradient: ten metres. Each of us stacks the bricks into individual towers of 250 bricks each. For every 1,000 bricks, you get eighty rubles. I brought up 250 bricks in twelve hours and when I got home I boasted to my mother that I'd earned twenty rubles. The work went pretty smoothly. Between us, Lithuanian and Finnish backs carried out whole mountains of bricks, boards, wooden strips and hoops for making barrels and even large and small fishing boats with oars. For a time, the Lithuanians lived under the rowing boats, propped up by planks, just to get out of the wind. The Finns sought shelter in dark, windowless tents made out of American flour sacks, which did not protect them from wind or rain.

Their tents and lean-tos were full of sick people, who were lying on the damp tundra completely neglected and dying. Typhus caught up with the Lithuanians too. Legions of lice marched over our outer clothing. It was September. The surface of the tundra got colder by the day. It would soon freeze and then the first blizzards would arrive.

Everyone alive is put to work on construction. A log hospital and a huge brick building are going up. There are tens of thousands of construction logs floating near the shore. They should have been dragged onto dry land, but there was no one to do it.

An infirmary is set up in a minuscule tent, a place for the Russian doctor to receive patients. But there is nowhere to admit them for treatment. Often the patients collapse on arrival, too feeble to drag themselves back to the barracks.

There is no bakery. Each of us is allotted 350 grams of flour. But where to bake or boil it? We go back to cooking on campfires and small outdoor fireplaces.

The brick structure we are preparing to build will be gigantic. We clear an area 25 metres by 150 and immediately begin to lay out a foundation. We work as architects and engineers, overseers and labourers. We place the bricks for the outside walls directly on the hard tundra, which has already been blanketed with snow. The top ten centimetres of tundra have by now frozen solid. What lies below is permafrost that never melts; even a summer burial requires hacking a grave out of ice. We make the walls fifty centimetres thick. We also brick out the interior walls that

43

will separate each room from the next. Layers of brick, layers of moss, layers of brick, layers of moss – that's what passes for architecture here. We fetch the moss from 500 metres away. We yank it out of the tundra with our hands and carry it in sacks on our backs. In the process, our skin peels off and our fingers turn numb and unresponsive. There's a low hill nearby where the dead are carted by a nag that's half dead himself. Initially, not many deportees died, only several a day, so that it was still possible to honour the dead by burying them in a grave, as befits human beings. When I run to fetch the moss, I'm cold. I have no felt leggings or padded Siberian trousers. I work in silk stockings, regular street shoes, a short dress and a summer coat that I brought from Lithuania but have already outgrown. Such are my work clothes, which are not unlike those of any other Lithuanian here. But when I heave the bag of moss onto my back and carry it to the building site, I warm up. In fact, building a dwelling place in which I will actually be able to live is oddly satisfying. The red-brick walls go up quickly. Once they're up, the construction phase is done. We move into one of the barrack rooms. We bring in boards to build pallets along the entire length of three walls; the fourth is reserved for the door and two mean windows. We have no ceiling. We use planks, which we position overhead to serve as both ceiling and a flat roof. Finally we toss about fifteen centimetres of moss over the planks, along with some soil, and we are ready to begin our new lives. The room is large: approximately eight metres wide and twenty-five metres long. Our entire covered wagon has been reunited again. Since space on the pallets is tight, Krikštanis, in his constant pursuit of fairness, allocates each of us fifty centimetres. That gives our family of three a total of one and a half metres. Now some rags to cover the pallets and, finally, we have shelter from the wind. But not the rain.

We place a small stove in the middle of the room. It is actually half an empty kerosene drum. We cut out an opening for firewood. Then we place the iron drum on the floor, open end down, insert a pipe at the top, make a hole in the ceiling and, after chopping up some construction boards we'd stolen earlier, we light a fire. A house-warming. The iron drum turns red hot, the dry boards crackle. The air in the barracks is thick with the stench of foot-wraps and damp clothes that haven't dried out in a month and are now beginning to disintegrate.

There are about twenty such rooms in this brick structure, inhabited by Finns, Lithuanians and Yakuts. It is a tight squeeze for us all.

We can feel winter coming. Our supervisors are in a hurry to salvage the logs that are still in the river, which has already begun to freeze near the shore, while, little by little, snow has begun to blanket the tundra. We pull the logs out of the river and onto the beach. The water is so frigid that it burns. Clothes that get wet become stiff, gloves turn hard as stone. We work without rest, because once we stop we immediately grow rigid from the cold. Two people from each brigade work in thigh-high rubber boots. They stand in the water and roll the logs towards us;

we in turn roll them onto the beach. Our clothes become soaked and splattered with mud. Several fishing boats anchored nearby are being packed with enormous fishing nets, tents, foodstuffs, equipment and oars. Four newly organized Lithuanian brigades are sailing to Sardach to fish. The fishermen climb aboard and set off quietly. My brother waves goodbye. What kind of fishing can there be when the river is about to fill with ice floes?

The tail end of the convoy has arrived: two huge barges packed with American goods. We work day and night unloading their riches. On the shore, next to the mountains of boards and bricks, enormous piles begin to appear, stacked with white American sacks, casks of butter and boxes of tinned food. The men carry two sacks each. A flour sack is also placed on my back. I take a step forward. I grow faint. I feel sharp pains, like a knife slashing across my abdomen. I realize I'm swaying. When I come to, I'm lying on the deck. The sack of flour has dislocated my shoulder as it fell.

'How old are you?'

'Fifteen.'

'Fifteen! And you can't lift a sack of flour? We have twelve-year-olds who can load ships. The masses have gone soft.'

The supervisor orders me to carry boxes of tins instead. The barge rocks back and forth, the gangplank sways – it is covered with ice and slippery underfoot – the boxes are heavy, awkward, and I have a pain in my gut. I carry my load up the riverbank, place it in a pile and head back down. At the bottom of the hill, I see two pallid Lithuanians cramming food into their mouths. They have slashed open a box of tins with a knife, then stashed the opened box back into the pile. As if by accident, sacks rip open, out spill flour, barley, sugar and peas, and casks of butter shatter. We eat the peas, stuff flour into our pockets and return frequently to the barracks to 'warm ourselves'. By the end of the day, using only our gloves and pockets, each of us has brought home between two and three kilos of flour and barley. Hidden behind a beam on one of the barges, a Lithuanian woman is filling up on flour, which will turn into raw dough in her mouth. But it's food. People are taking advantage of whatever comes to hand. Later, walking home in the evening, I notice two white sacks under the gangplank. Someone will be picking them up later that night. The barge is empty. The stockroom supervisor, the Estonian Kespaiko, notices the sacks but turns a blind eye. He was very clear, after all, when he told us, 'Take it, while it's still on the barge. Once it's on shore, I'm responsible for it, and there will be no stealing. Just beware of the skipper.'

The steamer tows the empty barges two kilometres to Konstantinovka, where the initial processing of the fish takes place – the 'fish factory', as we call it. We are being sent there to load up the produce. We begin moving the heavy barrels to the deck of the barge. But what we see in Konstantinovka leaves us stunned. The work station there consists of nothing but tables under the open sky and Finnish women gutting fish with their frozen and bleeding hands. The wind is bitter and it's blowing snow, but they continue gutting. 'Are you cold?' I ask. 'Yes, cold,' reply the Finns. 'Very cold.'

Though we work briskly loading barrels, we can't seem to get warm. Our fingers grow numb in our tattered gloves and we can't feel our legs. It is now snowing hard. A blizzard. But there is no end to the barrels. Finally, we're done. Now how do we get back to the barracks? We can't even see the river; everything has vanished in the whirlwind. We hear the whistle of the steamship, the sound of barges crushing the ice along the riverfront. The last convoy is leaving Trofimovsk. We get one more glimpse of our snow-covered barrels, then everything disappears in the blizzard. One or two days more and the river will stop flowing. We shall be completely cut off from the world, trapped in an alien environment. Guided by sheer instinct, I run along what I imagine to be the shore. Milė Noreikienė runs ahead. She has wrapped herself in a shawl to protect herself from the driving snow, which can scorch a face. We sink into the snow – and then into the water beneath. We pull out our feet and, with our legs now shackled in ice up to the knees, we run and run. Poor Milė, who loves to joke about and is always trying to cheer me up, pulls her foot out of her oversized man's shoe. Her foot is nearly bare – the foot-wraps have been carelessly tied – and her red heel glows in the snow. I burst out laughing and continue to run. It's painfully, excruciatingly cold. My thighs and my knees feel as if they're being pinched by the frigid air. Oh, God, help keep us safe, don't let us die. Polar winter has arrived!

I leave our barracks to attend to a 'call of nature'. The barracks next door stands empty, a bare brick shed without windows or roof. I climb in through the window frame and find myself a sheltered corner. The snow is well above my knees. Suddenly, I trip over something. I bend down to look. It's a naked woman, a Finn, covered with snow. I recoil in shock and trip again. I want to run but I'm rooted to the spot. There are corpses everywhere, naked legs and breasts, frozen hair poking out through the snow. Like blocks of wood, the bodies have frozen solid in every conceivable posture – hands and legs bent or outstretched, petrified at the moment of death. I stumble as I make for the window to escape this morgue of horrors. Meanwhile, snowflakes pirouette gracefully onto the bellies and sightless eyes of the dead. And to think that it's only autumn, that winter has barely begun. I wonder what is waiting for us ahead. How many of us will survive?

Our first killer winter in the Arctic is that of 1942–3. There are 450 Lithuanians at the mouth of the Lena River.

The last rays of the sun disappear in November, polar night takes over and the monstrous blizzards arrive in a furious dance of death. Although we have a brick shelter, we might as well be outside. The blizzards send the moss and soil flying from the roof. The boards howl and soon the blizzard will be tearing them off as well. Gaps have begun to appear between the boards and the snow comes whistling in through the cracks, covering us with a thick blanket. Filled with damp wood shavings, our mattresses freeze to the pallets. I cover myself with everything I have. I snuggle against my mother and breathe under the covers. This feels warm. Our snow blanket does not melt and provides warmth. The wind rips the door off its hinges and blows a mound of snow into the room. The walls ice over. Everyone is silent, though awake. It feels like morning.

'Mum, do you think Zagurski has opened the store yet? Maybe he's got bread?'

'Shut up, damn you.' I hear Noreikienė's voice. 'Yesterday's ration was supposed to last us two days and we've eaten it already.'

'But, Mum, maybe someone will give us just a little bit?'

'So go and ask. Maybe they will.'

I am upset. There won't be any work today, but neither do I feel like lying here doing nothing. I slide out quickly from under my rags, shake the snow from my foot-wraps and in a flash slip my feet into my felt boots – ripped and soleless leftovers from our time in the Altai territory. I wrap the smelly sacks that never dry out tightly around the tops of my boots and secure them with rope. I pull on my thin, padded trousers and the jacket my brother has outgrown. 'Hundred-threads' comes last – a jacket that's been padded using an old bathrobe and cotton batting. I sigh with pleasure. Those still lying on their pallets, too timid to crawl out from under their rags, which by now have become thick with condensation, envy me, I know. Hurriedly, Krikštanis also pulls on his trousers. Together, we paw at the snow with our hands, hoping to clear an opening where the door used to be that is large enough to crawl through. After an hour's effort, we manage to make a hole near the top of the doorway. I stretch out on my stomach and continue working. Finally, I am able to jam my legs against the upper frame – but still no contact with the outside. We've been plugged solid. But I can feel the snow getting lighter; I can even feel it quivering from the storm outside. One more punch and my hand breaks through the wall of snow. Just as I'm about to yell, 'Made it!' to Krikštanis the blizzard kicks me in the face, shuts my eyes, bursts down my throat, up my sleeves and through my gloves. My eyelashes ice over, my eyelids freeze shut and I crawl back inside gasping for air. I fall face down on the floor and breathe deeply. My heart pounds. In no time, the blizzard plugs up my narrow tunnel again. But Krikštanis and I quickly push our way through and find ourselves in the open air. It's blowing a hurricane outside. Visibility is about one and a half steps and the wind is fierce. It knocks us down instantly, we topple over each other. Side by side, we face the elements, crawling on our hands and knees, sometimes on our stomachs. We lean our heads into the wind to keep it from snatching our breath away. Even so, I gasp for air and my heart pounds.

Seizing whatever log or block of ice lies in our path, we inch forward. I like this all-out battle with the elements. I clench my teeth and, centimetre by centimetre, make headway against the fury of the blizzard. My gloved hands grow numb, my knees feel wooden inside my padded trousers. Never mind – I'll thaw out later. The snow that blew in through the slit in my trousers feels like a cold compress on my body. We seem to have been at it for several hours. Finally, we reach the stockroom with the boards. We select five long construction boards each, then get up and run. The wind is now at our backs and, with boards for wings, we find ourselves airborne. I have trouble staying on my feet. I slip and fall on my spoils, I get up and run on. Yet I feel like laughing. We reach our barracks, or to be precise we reach its flat roof with the short chimney pipes protruding through the snow. To locate our room in the barracks, we count the chimneys and begin to scoop out an opening. Although our hole has been plugged, the snow is soft and, one by one, we thrust the boards into the room. Then it's our turn. Krikštanis goes first, but his shoulders are wide. He gets stuck above the door frame, half in, half out, with his legs still out in the snow. Finally, his legs disappear with the rest of him and seconds later we're both inside. It takes only a few minutes to get the thick boards crackling happily in the fire and the iron sides of the drum and the vent red-hot and glowing. Our situation begins to feel less horrifying. Krikštanis and I unwind the sacks and foot-wraps from our legs and begin to dry ourselves out. I use an empty tin to boil some water and bring it to my mother and brother. But the hot water just stirs our insides to life and our hunger becomes even less bearable. If only it were twelve o'clock already. I contemplate the prospect of spending the day in the frigid barracks, which an entire stockroom of boards couldn't heat. By the flickering light of our kindling, we can see each other's jaundiced, grimy, sooty faces, our sunken, famished eyes. The same hunger is etched into all of our faces: the hunger for bread.

Each morning we emerge from our barracks in single file and inch across the *zavod* grounds. We move slowly because the sacks wrapped around our feet get in the way. Nor do we have the energy for speed. We proceed downhill to the shore. Huge stacks of logs stretch all the way to Konstantinovka. About a third of them remain icebound in the river. Our brigade consists of Daniliauskas, Totoraitis, his daughter, Štarienė, Nausėdienė and me. Krikštanienė is our 'brigadier', our team leader.

The stacks of logs are covered with a thick layer of snow and there is no sign of the pits we made yesterday, from which to extract logs. They've been completely levelled by the blizzard. We search for our sledges, shovels and crowbars. We find the sledges buried in snow. After clearing our work site and shovelling out the stacks, we tear at the logs with crowbars. Some medium-sized logs have been laid vertically against the sides of the pit, creating a surface that makes the job of extraction easier. Once a log has been extracted, we place one end on a small wooden sledge. Then, hitched four to a sledge, we all pull on command to get it moving. If the logs aren't very thick – about twenty centimetres in diameter – we haul two at a time. Sometimes, when they're very thick – forty or fifty centimetres each – we can barely handle one. '*Raz, dva, vzyali!*' – 'One, two, heave!' At Krikštanienė's command, we lean forward and heave. The ropes are taut against our shoulders – strained to breaking point – but the sledge does not budge. We try again. Again, lips pursed, ropes taut, we strain to move the sledge forward – again nothing, except the snapping of a rope and Antanas Daniliauskas taking a nosedive onto the ice. Blood stains his upper lip. Eventually, we get the sledge to move and begin towing it up the riverbank. We pull it along a track of ice about a metre wide. This makes the uphill journey less arduous. We walk on either side of the track, keeping the ropes taut, to stop the log from sliding back downhill. The rope slices into my shoulder like a knife. I can feel the throbbing of blood in my temples and at my neck. We're only halfway up the hill, yet I'm at the end of my strength. I'm already bent double, my hands hanging so low they're nearly grazing the ground. One more step, one more… The rope presses into my left shoulder. I feel a constriction in my chest – like a hellish pair of pliers squeezing my heart. Everything begins to sway – the snow, the hill – and then… a blur. God, help me pull this log up the hill, just this one. One more step, then another… Finally. We're at the summit. We straighten, we rest. Gradually, everything comes back into focus, the pain in my heart subsides. I wonder how the others feel. Do they also get that gut-wrenching, heart-crushing feeling with each step they take? Probably not; they're stronger, they're mature. Not in vain did Krikštanienė warn me, when she chose me to work in her brigade, that I'd have to pull my weight. Her brigade was not obliged to cover the children's share too. I was not to work any less, pull any less, lift any less, for the brigade's income would be shared equally among us.

We get up and haul the logs onto a pile. We lift each log from the sledge and together hoist them up so they're three deep. Again a sharp pain in the gut. But only for a moment. Pulling the empty sledge behind us, we head back downhill. How good that feels, if only the moment could last. How effortless without ropes.

We jostle out two more logs, lift them from the pit and with great difficulty position them on the sledge. Again, like a pair of pliers, the rope squeezes my chest, my back. Again and again and again. If only things moved faster, faster, faster. Again the throbbing of blood, the slipping of legs, the thrust of pain in the abdomen. If only I could grow up this instant. Perhaps then the work would be less agonizing. The days drag on. Each is inhumanly long and hard. At one o'clock, we throw down our tools and stagger to lunch. That is the happiest moment of our day. I wait for it, I dream of it in my sleep! A cup of hot water and a chunk of aromatic bread with a distinctive, crunchy crust. I slip into the barracks and by the light of some kindling I see my mother lying on the pallet. Beside her lie two chunks of bread – mine and my brother's. I feel dizzy with joy but also faint. My mouth waters at the sight but I control myself. I untie the ropes and unwind the icy sacks from my feet. I roll the chunk of bread around in my hands – the day's ration. For a moment, at least, I want to prolong the pleasure. But my hands and legs are shaking. One more second and my teeth sink into this incredibly delicious bread. I chew for a long time and drink some water. 'Mama, was cake really delicious? Did

it taste better than bread, do you think?' The faint light
of kindling flickers in the pitch-black darkness of the barracks. Twenty-five people, their eyes focused on a single
spot, are eating. I notice my mother's eyes, suddenly lit
by a spark from the stick in her hands. They're very deep
and full of pain.

'Mama, Mama, my one, my only precious darling
mother, we will live, we will survive, we will return. We
will, Mama. Oh, Mama, I promise!'

A school with seven grades opens on 1 December. I am
placed in the seventh grade. To earn my ration of bread,
I haul logs until noon – just four hours. At twelve o'clock,
I feel reborn. Everyone goes for lunch. I too take off my
rope, drag my enormous, sack-wrapped feet into the barracks, fortify myself, grab my briefcase and Krikštanis's
inkwell, and run to class.

Buried in the snow are two small houses: our school. I
walk into my class and am greeted by my wonderful classmates. They offer me a place by the iron stove. I unwind
the ropes and sacks from my feet and stick them under
the desk. I tear off the scarf that has frozen to my face
and brush the ice from my lashes. The classroom is tiny,
just four shared desks and a small table for the teacher.
The bell rings and we take our seats. There are six of us.
I'm sitting at the desk in the front row with Tautvilas
Stasiūnas. Behind us – the Finn, Kekonen, sits with the
Yakut, Semionov; and the two Yakut girls, Pticeva and
Trochova, sit together.

The teacher is speaking. She smells of fresh lumber, the woods and something else I can't place. A pleasant warmth spreads over my body – God, how I wish the lesson would never end and that we did not have to return to the dark cave. I'm overcome by sleep. Logs appear before my eyes. The open sore on my shoulder stings. Forty-five minutes fly by like five. Why did lessons feel so long in secondary school? Russian grammar is beyond my comprehension. Algebra is also difficult. I really belong in the sixth grade.

'*Vy krepko pozabyli elementy algebralnykh deystvy – ne uprazhnyaytes. Vspomnite.*' – 'You've forgotten quite a bit of your algebra. You've not been practising. Try to remember.' She admonishes me kindly.

I'm standing at the blackboard in my torn felt boots and filthy padded work trousers with a piece of chalk in my hand, wondering, how did I get here? I must be dreaming. The place is warm, there are candles, light, I'm being addressed as a person: '*Vy pozabyli.*' – 'You've forgotten it.' Yet I can still hear the other voice: 'Get up, damn you. If you can't do the work, get out of the brigade.' I am lifting the end of a log, when suddenly I feel faint and the log drops to the ground. I hear cursing… My school days flash before my eyes. I sit here dazed. For heaven's sake, Dalia, wake up, look alive, you're in class again. Slowly, I come round. My situation is not that odd, after all. During the break, the six of us sit around the stove and each tells his or her story. My classmates are kind; they pity me, as I do them. They're famished, as I am. The lice, which have thawed out indoors, crawl down their backs, as they do down mine. They too scratch and fidget constantly. They will soon return to their cold and dark caves, as I will, and shiver all night under their lice-infested rags. Like me, they will wait for one o'clock tomorrow afternoon, when they will once again be able to return to a warm schoolroom. Lessons end for the day. To draw out the moment in this Eden, we idle, we let our foot-wraps dry a little longer near the stove, we take our time wrapping the sacks around our feet, we tie on our muzzles. That's the rag or scarf that covers the face, exposing only our eyes. On the school doorstep, the blizzard tears Pticeva's notebook out of her hand and, howling madly, flings it at the sky. We run through the snowdrifts, we stumble, the blizzard knocks us off our feet.

Pressing my book bag – Daddy's briefcase – to my chest, I crawl home from school. The wind hammers at my head, whips my face, glues my eyelashes together, clamps them shut so tightly that I can't open my eyes. I pull my hand out of my glove and tear the ice from my lashes. The beastly blizzard is in a rage. A little further, yes, this must be the hole. I scoop out the opening into the barracks, stretch out on my stomach and slide down. I hit the door with my head. That's it. I'm 'home'. School recedes like a dream. In the dark, with my eyes glued shut and my bear-sized legs covered in ice, I trip over someone's bucket. Oh, the stench. I head for my bunk, trip over something else – for which I get an elbow in the chest and fall. Krikštanis, Adolis Ašmantas, Kazlauskas and Žukienė are sitting at the dying fire. There is no room for anyone else.

Krikštanis's eyes blaze with hunger like a dog's. A piece of kindling glows in his hand. He lights his cigarette, and for a second I can see his soot- and stubble-covered face, the hollow cheeks and sunken eyes.

'I have to say, my friends, that the hard-labour prison in Kaunas was like a health resort. A kilo of bread per day and some hot stew. We got a large bowl of thick and meaty soup with so much fat floating on top that it kept the steam from rising. And a second course. Also meat. A large serving, honestly, a decent-sized portion. I have to say, you could really fill up on it.'

Silence. The conversations are a torment. Everyone fantasizes. Starvation causes an already diseased imagination to hallucinate. At night, we all dream of bread (the first law of hunger), but when you go to eat it – the bread disappears. You wake up with your head on fire and a mouth full of saliva. 'Today, I dreamt that I was eating a hearty loaf of farmer's bread, and do you know how much I polished off...?'

He's lying, the snake; he just saw it in his dream but did not get to taste it, because it always disappears. But it's still a pleasure to listen to comments about bread, so we let him go on, even though no one believes him. Kazlauskas can paint some pretty fantastic images of food. He's psychologically unstable. He was deported by mistake. Starvation in the labour camp probably affected his mind. Upon his release, he joined his wife in the Altai territory, only to be deported with her to the Far North. En route, he ate all day – bartered things for food and ate and ate and ate.

He hadn't fully recovered when he ended up here to starve again. Interesting too is the fact that more than once he regretted joining his wife. He'd say, 'The penal camp was easier than this.' Hitched solo to his little cart, he delivers firewood to the supervisors by day. When he gets his ration of bread, he devours it right there in the store, without ever leaving the counter. If it's the butter ration for the month, he'll eat that too, by itself, all at once. Same with sugar. On one occasion, Kazlauskas was sitting next to Krikštanis and holding a chunk of frozen fish in his hands. He held it against the stove to defrost it but, too impatient to wait, he began to eat it. Fish guts dangled from the corners of his mouth, blood ran down his hands, while he chomped away noisily and shuddered. Now and then, his ghostly eyes would flash in the dark while he ate. Five minutes later, there was nothing left. Kazlauskas had eaten the scales, the tail and the bloody entrails smeared with excrement. He never even thought to boil the fish. I think Krikštanis finds Kazlauskas entertaining. Kazlauskas will even steal the sledge dogs' rations, after they've been unhitched and are being fed. But stealing food from a starving dog that's pulled sledges all day is no easy matter. Kazlauskas's face is often bloody after an encounter with the dogs. 'You know, I never really ate my fill in Lithuania either. How can you ever feel full? No matter how much you eat, you still want more. Ha, ha, ha.' The man's unhinged, he's hallucinating. Imagine... starving in Lithuania! His small, slight frame shivers as he talks, he rubs his hands and laughs quietly, his clothes reek of urine.

'I don't understand you, Krikštanis. Here you are, a cultured man, yet you talk like a low life,' Žukienė says, patronizingly.

'Well, if it isn't the countess,' mocks the democrat. 'Why shouldn't I say it, when Erich Remarque himself wrote it?'

'Your Remarque was a cynic, sir.'

'Remarque – the great realist – a cynic? If Remarque is a cynic, then you, madam, are an ass and understand absolutely nothing about politics or literature.'

'Karl Kautsky once said, "Goodbye to famine and hunger, we've just discovered noodle soup." But we speak as we live: enough said.' Žukienė gets the last word.

It is pitch black in the barracks. Everyone is lying down, ulcerated legs bent at the knees. I would love to curl up and lie still, but then I won't be able to straighten my legs in the morning. I'd have to unbend my rigid knees by hand and lower them manually to the ground. The pain would be heart-stopping. So, instead, I sit in my space on the pallet between Prapuolenienė and my mother, light my tallow candle, which I stole from school, and do my homework. As the snow from the ceiling begins to thaw from the candle's heat, it drips down the back of my neck. My hands are numb and I am shivering. I'm doing algebra. My friends, my teachers, my school days appear like a mirage in the room. The candle sputters. My head droops towards my knees. The icy barracks with its lice, its hunger, its cold, its stench of human waste fades into the darkness. I slide into the narrow space between the two bodies and visions of my childhood appear like images on a screen. I stare at the dark and yearn to be comforted. I want to snuggle up to someone. I want moral support. I want someone strong to lean on. I don't want to feel alone. I want to be consoled. I snuggle against my mother, reach over to kiss her – and feel her face wet with tears.

'Mama, Mama, I'll be graduating from school in the spring and I've got permission to attend a technical college in Yakutsk. I'll get you out of here, Mama. You've got to believe me, we'll break out of here yet, Mama, I promise.'

My mother's hand strokes my hair.

'Broniuk, I don't know about anyone else, but we'll survive.' I can hear Krikštanis's voice. 'We're young, we're strong, we'll manage somehow. Grinkevičienė, Atkočaitienė, maybe not – they're feeble, sick – but we'll endure. We have to endure.'

Someone is urinating into a tin can, then climbing back into the bunk. Nausėdienė's cigarette glows in the dark.

Death, along with famine, typhus, lice, scurvy and frigid temperatures, has wormed its way into our ghastly barracks. The infirmary set up in the barracks next door is overflowing with the sick and the dying. It is more like a morgue. Those dying from typhus are laid out on bare, snow-covered boards. Most are delirious. Vidoklerienė, whose son died yesterday and has been placed naked in the doorway, is shrieking, '*Akasha, pochemu ty mne pokhoronny marsh igrayesh?*' – 'Akasha, why are you playing the funeral march for me?' The blizzard has long since buried the door to the infirmary. The small stove is out. The wind is driving the snow in through the chimney pipe and the stove is quaking and bellowing with the wind. Complete darkness. The sick do not feel the cold, they're burning up. Some are unconscious and some – they're already on the other side.

For three days no one has entered the infirmary; the door is blocked by a mountain of snow. For four whole days there has been no food, no medicine, not a drop of water or a stick of firewood. The dead lie alongside the living. The sole nurse cannot lift the corpses from their pallets. She just goes from patient to patient, checking who is still alive. Balčiuvienė calls for her husband. She gasps for air, makes gurgling noises. Her small daughter is lying next to her and cradles her mother's head: 'Mama, Mama, don't die, Mama…'

'Dear God Almighty, have mercy. Have mercy on these people, take pity on the sick, stop this blizzard…' I can hear the nurse's hair-raising shrieks, as she kneels to pray inside the morgue, and her hysterical wailing: 'Oh, my God. Oh, my God…' I can feel her body tremble in the dark and hear her lamentations over the death rattles and the roar of the storm.

Our barracks has been illuminated. A candle stands on either side of Atkočaitienė's corpse – two whole candles – which means that someone has been stealing candles from the town office and hoarding them. Her nose seems absurdly long. It dominates her waxen, soot-covered, ema-ciated face, which is crawling with lice. I've never seen so many lice – entire divisions march across her nose, her eyelids, her lips, then disappear into her neighbour's rags. Taking advantage of the candlelight, I stand there reading the history of the Middle Ages.

Yesterday, I sat facing the open doors of the stove in order to study. No one could deny me that warm and well-lit spot, because it was my stolen boards burning inside. Everyone maintained a respectful silence. By the light of the flames, I could see Atkočaitienė preparing soup from her ration of bread, then helping herself to the bread simmering in the pot next to hers, in which Kazlauskienė was boiling 200 grams of bread in two litres of water. I grasped her hand and said to her, 'Aren't you ashamed, a devout Catholic like yourself?' Atkočaitienė grabbed her cup of soup and slid over to her bunk, where she began to eat greedily. All you could hear in the dark was her slurping.

Just yesterday this devout woman was making such a show of singing hymns and rattling her rosary beads in the silence of the barracks that even Ari, listening to her pray, asked his father, 'Daddy, where is God?'

'There is no God, Ari,' thundered the 'emperor's' voice in the icy darkness of the barracks.

'God, have mercy on his soul, for he knows not what he says,' we heard Atkočaitienė mumble to herself.

Today, Stefanija Jasinskienė notices that some of her grain is missing, grain she herself had stolen from the Altai beetroot farm. With the help of some lighted kindling, she sees a scattering of grain next to Atkočaitienė's pallet.

Jasinskienė grabs a switch and begins to whip the elderly Atkočaitienė's face and hands. The old woman falls to her knees and beats her breast protesting her innocence, but the merciless blows continue to fall on her shoulders. We tear the switch from Jasinskienė's hand. Atkočaitienė confesses and Jasinskienė forgives her. She even kisses the old woman on the face, though it's swarming with lice.

Abromaitis's charnel brigade arrives and Atkočaitienė exits feet first out of the barracks. Žukienė takes possession of her candles and motions for me to take Atkočaitienė's place on the pallet. Done.

I'm sitting at the stove with Krikštanis. 'I have to say, Dalia, you're incredibly determined, practically possessed, in the way you grapple with life,' he tells me. My heart leaps with pleasure at the compliment. The young Totoraitis girl climbs down from her bunk and, turning her back to us, seats herself on the pail. She suffers from dysentery, her diarrhoea is constant. Ten times a day she sits on the pail, exposing her posterior. The pail is full, smelly. Her mother, unable to get outside because the blizzard has plugged the opening, pours the foul waste into the snow that has blown into the room. We have no other water, so we rely on the snow in the barracks. We melt it in a can and drink it.

Half the boards in the stockroom are now gone. Everyone steals, because there is no firewood to be found nearby and no one has the strength to haul it in from a kilometre away. Our stove crackles, our boards crackle. We roll our trousers up in front of the fire, clean away the pus and pick the lice from the sores on our shins. The lice like to congregate in wounds but they produce a terrible itch. The wounds do not heal – they haven't for several months – and every evening our trousers have to be prised from the open wounds to which they've become glued. It is a painful but bearable procedure.

The barracks is awash with light. Almost everyone is in possession of some splinter of wood or a candle and engaged in nit-picking. It's an ethically satisfying activity: you bite me, I crush you back. Between the thumbnails. Lice are easy to find in shirts, harder in sweaters and therefore twice as satisfying when they're found. Little by little, we've become quite expert in this. At night, we pick off the lice in the dark and throw them into a glass. In the morning, we toss the contents outside through the hole in the snow. Jasinskienė has perfected a technique that is even more basic. She chews each louse that she catches right on the spot and spits it out. Grockis, who is also sick and lies next to her day and night, says that he can hear her grinding lice in her teeth around the clock. It is getting on his nerves. Jasinskienė is suffering from scurvy, so her legs have seized up. She can't straighten them out. That means a field day for lice, which prefer their victims lying down. When we lived in the Altai territory, she was the strongest woman there: she carried sacks that weighed 100 kilos. Now she's been forced to sell her two-year-old daughter's ration card in order to purchase a single card for herself, which will have to feed them both. They've already finished the grain, for which she beat Atkočaitienė, and will have to survive on 600 grams of bread. Dalia, her daughter, wets herself. So Jasinskienė asked me to hang the child's sweater and underwear up to dry, which I did, but someone swiped them. Now the woman sobs helplessly. She can't get off the pallet. She wets and soils herself as well, then shivers in the sodden and foul rags, snuggling against her toddler's tiny body to keep warm. Grockis has dysentery, but still has the strength to get up and use the bucket. Juozas and Oldas are bedridden with frostbite on their feet. In our barracks, only a few of us remain upright; one of them is me.

My mother is sick. Her whole head has swollen up. She weighs no more than thirty kilos and looks like a girl. Her ribs stick out and her legs are so thin that they're nothing but skin over bones. She seems light enough for me to lift and carry outside in my arms. She has a fever and she can't see anything because her eyes are swollen too. Juozas and I sit there watching her. Our terrible fear draws us closer together. Then we hug each other and weep.

'Dalia, if Mama dies I'm going to kill myself with this knife,' says my brother, who is lying on his stomach. I can feel his long, lean, debilitated body shaking with sobs.

Mum is already unconscious. For the first time since this nightmare began, I pray. 'Dear God, don't take my mother, don't take my mother,' I plead, while hugging her unresponsive body, which has become no more than a skeleton, and her red, horribly deformed, swollen face.

Someone is shovelling his way into our cave. He slides in and announces in a loud voice that the trial has begun; they're just waiting for me. I emerge from my covers, as does Žukienė, who is attending as a witness.

'Goodbye, Mama, goodbye.' I kiss her unconscious body, her face, her hands, her feet.

Juozas and I know what has happened. We understand. Mum has condemned herself to death by starvation; she would divide her ration in two and discreetly slip the two pieces of bread to us. Starving creatures that we were, frozen and brutalized by the mountain of logs to which we were hitched every day, we would grab our share without asking, 'Mama, have you eaten?' We killed our mother, you and I; we're selfish brutes. What the world calls heroism is nothing compared to your strength, Mother, nothing compared to your love, to your heroic sacrifice. Matrasov, who covered the embrasure of a machine gun with his body, is a pygmy compared to you and your loving heart, which condemned you to a slow and painful death. A mother's heart! Goodbye, Mama. When I return from the trial, you will already be cold. It is better this way. You will be spared the sight of your daughter being led off to prison. Goodbye, Mama! Žukienė tears me away from my mother's body, which is still warm with life.

I am sitting in the dock along with the five others on trial for stealing boards from the stockroom. Across from us, at a table covered with red felt and lit by five candles, sits the magistrate, an eighteen-year-old Yakut. An inspector by profession, he has been ordered to preside by the Party, which must have deemed it inappropriate for a local man to play judge. The magistrate is flanked on each side by a secretary taking notes. On one side is Novikova from Leningrad, a teacher of draughtsmanship at the school and a member of the Young Communist League. On the other is Mironova, a higher-ranking member of the Young Communists. This one spends her days and nights entertaining supervisors. The trial chamber is just an empty barracks next door that serves as a sewing workshop by day. The two iron stoves are red hot, spreading warmth. My head is in a shambles: images and faces blur, my eyelids droop. I just want to sleep.

I hear the voice of Riekus as in a dream: 'No, that's not true, citizen magistrate, I did not steal. I had been making a coffin that day and took home only the leftover scraps of wood.'

Idiot, why defend yourself? What's the point of lying? What difference does it make where we die – in prison or in this majestic factory of death called Trofimovsk? My head drops to my chest as I'm overwhelmed by sleep. The room is filled with spectators and I hear a buzzing in the room, the drone of voices.

'That's not true, Judge, I didn't take that stick of wood. I did pick it up, but when I ran into Sventicki, I dropped it as soon as he yelled at me. I didn't bring home so much as a sliver.'

I tear open my eyes. It's the old Finn, who is about seventy years old, with the deeply sunken eyes of an abused

Dalia with her mother and brother, 1937.

dog. The face an artist might draw of famine. He had been in Leningrad during the blockade, where the daily ration had been 125 grams of bread made of chaff and clay. Then he was upgraded to Trofimovsk's factory of death (600 grams of bread, frigid weather, scurvy, typhus, lice and a polar winter). A felon, obviously. He has undermined the state. How dare he bring back some firewood to light the stove in his ghastly barracks – just to thaw his face and eyes, to dry his icy clothes, which are as hard as armour.

Facing us on the witness bench sits the Pole, Sventicki, that Judas with a double chin, smiling pudgy eyes and a snout that's never far from the trough. He sees the plundering of the boards, the vanishing wealth of the state. But the naked corpses that are dead as a result of their service to the state and stacked like logs outside our barracks – these he doesn't see. He doesn't see that we steal to stay alive. Or perhaps he does see, the swine. He's just a loyal cur, furthering his career on the backs of our dead bodies. I could sink my nails into his repulsive neck.

'I refute the charges. I did not steal. We found the icy board in the river – when our brigade was foraging for firewood – and so we brought it home. The entire brigade can testify to that.'

Nothing but lies. Markevičienė is lying. The brigade is lying. The entire Soviet state tells lies and will continue to lie in perpetuity. It stole, it steals and it will steal. The other five defendants all deny the charges. Behind me, I can hear the crowd murmuring in approval. It will soon be my turn.

A week ago, I came home from school and found my mother was too weak to get up. She was begging everyone for water, but no one had a drop. I fished around in the dark and located the bucket, which still had several bits of ice sticking to the bottom from the snow we had melted the day before. By now almost everyone was bedridden. So Žukienė lit her stick of kindling and said to me, 'Light the stove, Dalia. Bring back some boards and we'll melt water for your mother. You'll feel warmer yourself and I want some soup. No one has lit the stove today. The sick haven't had any water. There is no one else to do it. Krikštanienė has been standing in a queue for several hours, waiting for bread.'

I slide out of the barracks. It's quiet outside, profoundly quiet, even eerie. Not only is there no blizzard, there's not even a breeze, just an immobilizing cold that has turned everything to ice – the river mouth, the tundra, the barracks, us. The northern lights have illuminated the sky; it's bright out, which is a bad thing. Stealing is going to be tough tonight. I sneak over to the depot, slip through the fence and grab three marvellously thick boards. The snow crunches underfoot. Alerted by my footsteps, a guard wrapped in a dog pelt heads in my direction. I let go of the boards, drop face down in the snow and press myself flat against the tundra. I raise my head. 'Dog Pelt' has turned back. I give him or her the finger and thrust the boards through the fence. In the blink of an eye, I'm on the other side, crawling with one end of each board tucked firmly under my armpits and the other end dragging in the snow.

The minutes seem like hours. Faster, faster! Ah, here we are, our palace of a barracks – I've reached the first corner of the red-brick building. But my energy is gone. I feel dizzy and ravenously hungry. I suck, I bite my lips, stuff my mouth with snow, chew, but my hunger does not go away.

Yet what splendour above. The northern lights are a magnificent web of colour. We are surrounded by grandeur: the immense tundra, as ruthless and infinite as the sea; the vast Lena estuary backed up with ice; the colossal, 100-metre-pillar caves on the shores of Stolby; and the aurora borealis. Against a background of such majesty, we are the pitiful things here – starved and infested like dogs, and nearly done in, rotting in our befouled and stinking ice caves.

Something is moving ahead of me. A creature not of this world – nothing but bones, the Grim Reaper. She is picking through the cesspit of the fifth barracks, looking for something to eat. Idiot, what do you think you're going to find? What do you think people are throwing away? Crazed with hunger, they'll soon be devouring their own fingers.

Here we are – our barracks. Quick as a flash, I fling the boards inside. I chop them up and get the stove going. It turns red hot in no time. We melt some snow, give it to the sick and they salt it and drink. I spoon hot tea into my mother's mouth. She doesn't have the strength to speak. Male and female have become indistinguishable, just bones, bones and more bones. Suddenly, Sventicki appears. He lights his candle. The construction boards are crackling in the fire and the rest lie chopped in a pile.

'Who stole the boards?'

Silence.

'Who chopped these boards?' the always proper but cunning Pole enquires pleasantly.

Silence.

I pull the covers over my mother and slide off the bunk.

'I did.'

'You?'

'Me.'

Just a few heads emerge from their rags. The rest are beyond caring. They don't react to anything any more. I'm afraid for my mother, but she doesn't know what's going on either. The charges are written up on the spot. Žukienė and I sign them.

'Will the accused citizen rise?'

I stand up. The magistrate observes my hideously wrapped feet, my tattered, padded trousers, the jacket made out of a dressing gown and my thick plaits, and, raising his narrow, piercing eyes, he looks directly into mine. The room falls silent. I see the school principal, Guliayev, the factory manager, Mavrin, and our emperor of food, Travkin. They're on the side bench whispering to each other. It is strangely quiet. I look the judge squarely in the eye. For about thirty seconds.

'How old are you?'

'Fifteen.'

He reads the charges. He reads for a long time. The candles on the red table flicker and shadows writhe on the red-brick walls. There's no ice on these walls. He reads and reads and reads. My legs tremble, as though they had weights on them. If only they'll let me sit down soon. Mama has probably died. They'll also be charging Juozas. He began cramming tinned food into his mouth during the autumn unloading right under the supervisors' noses. He suffers terribly from hunger, it's a lot harder for him than it is for me. Yesterday, he tried to get up and inch his way to the stove on his heels – he can't walk since his toes got frostbite – but he crashed full length on the floor and fainted. His handsome face looked very white in the darkness, his slender body practically weightless. Our mother is dead, Juozas will also die. He already has dysentery, and that's usually a ticket to the pile of cadavers outside. Suddenly, Mum's face appears before my eyes, as I remember it from childhood. Beautiful, gentle eyes, large curls on her forehead, a smile on her face. 'Mama, Mama, you're gone, you're growing cold even as I stand here. I should be there to close your eyes. Juozas, who is lying by your side, will weep helplessly when he realizes that you've grown cold. Why did you have to starve yourself for us, just to let us starve a little longer, die a lingering death, become a laughing stock in prison, which is where we'll be headed tomorrow? But I don't care. You're gone, and what happens tomorrow doesn't matter any more.' I hear someone talking to me. Suddenly, I find myself thinking, wouldn't it be great if someone at this very moment, right now, slowly, gently, took out his revolver and shot me. My body is giving out. I have just enough strength to wish for a quick death.

'I'm asking you a question, which you're obliged to answer.' A voice breaks through my fog and I finally comprehend what's being said. 'Do you agree to the charges and acknowledge that they are truthful?'

'Yes.'

A pause.

'Do you understand Russian well?'

'Yes.'

'Do you admit your guilt?'

'Yes.'

The magistrate looks confused. There is a din in the room. 'Stupid girl!' 'Child, defend yourself!'

'Will the defendant please answer the question thoughtfully. Do you admit that you stole boards from the stockroom?'

'Yes.'

Silence.

'And chopped them?'

'Yes.'

'Who put you up to it?'

Žukienė shuts her eyes and turns white as a sheet.

'No one.'

'You went on your own?'

'Yes, on my own.'

'Why did you steal?'

'To have something to burn.'

'Did you know that the boards are state property?'

'I did.'

'Were you aware that there's a penalty for stealing?'

'I was aware.'

'Do you realize what you're saying?'

'I do.'

'Where do you work?'

'I haul logs.'

'I'm told you attend school.'

'Yes, I also attend school.'

'What grade are you in?'

'Seventh.'

'Aren't you ashamed, you, a schoolgirl, to be sitting here on this bench?'

Silence. He repeats the question. The room is deathly still. At the back of the barracks, I hear someone crying softly – someone pities me. It's the voice of eleven-year-old Lialė Maknytė. For a moment, the room, the judge, the spectators, everything vanishes; a different scene takes its place. I had just turned fourteen. It was 28 May 1941. I was on my way to the theatre and in a hurry. I was taking a short cut through Vytautas Park and about to skip down the steps, when suddenly I stopped dead in my tracks, entranced by the sight before me. The sun was golden, the city aglow at my feet, the air smelt of blossoms. For the first time in my life, my heart throbbed with the joy of springtime, which was my springtime too. I took a deep breath, closed my eyes and felt incredibly happy. 'Ah, life, how splendid you are. And youth – how splendid too! What a joy to be alive!' My eyes, wide with excitement, welled up with tears of adolescent bliss and I headed full tilt down the hill, drawn by the siren call of the theatre, of music and the rapture of young life.

My eyes are open still, but I feel neither joy nor sadness. The tears are gone, they've dried up. I'm unable to cry. My beautiful vision of Vytautas Park has disappeared.

I feel the prying eyes of the room on me. They stare intently. Am I ashamed? Ashamed of giving my dying mother a drink of water? What is it you want to see, you Travkins, Mavrins and Sventickis? You gluttons. Is it remorse? Shame? But it's you who should be ashamed, you're the murderers, not me! I can hear the question being repeated.

'No, I am not at all ashamed.'

'Sit.'

I drop. I can hear the hum of voices. Someone is whispering in my ear, 'You've gone mad, girl. What have you done?' Žukienė is answering questions. I hear her say, 'No, that was the first time. She's never done anything like this before.'

Ha! Are you serious! First time! If you only knew, Sventicki! You could cover all the roofs of Trofimovsk with the boards I've stolen. You're such an ass. Haven't you figured out yet that we're on a tundra, that there are no forests here, no vegetation of any kind, and that even Neanderthals need fire. So what are we supposed to do? Gather the driftwood that washes ashore on the banks of the Lena? That's ten kilometres away! And just who do you expect to haul it in? The corpses lying under our bunks? The sick who have dysentery, who soil themselves on their pallets? Or do you have Jasinskienė in mind, the one with scurvy? The one with the twisted legs, who screams in pain?

The court leaves to deliberate. They deliberate a long time. I'm tormented by sleep, by exhaustion, by weakness. All I want to do is put my head down and sleep. I'm awakened by a sharp jab in my side: 'Get up, damn it!'

Riekus, Kobra and one other Lithuanian, I seem to remember, get two years apiece. As a minor who admitted her guilt, I am acquitted. I probably have my teacher Novikova to thank. What a blessing. To think that such good fortune has befallen me. Lialė kisses me and weeps, but this time with happiness. You have a beautiful soul, Lialė. But not for long. Life will prove a hard taskmaster and in time you will become less discriminating in choosing between good and evil, especially where others are concerned.

I tear at the entrance to our barracks and crawl in. I rush to the pallets. Silence. I stand there riveted and terrified. I hesitate to pull back the rags. But only for an instant. Then I climb onto the bunk and remove the covering from her face. She's breathing. Oh, God, she's breathing. I bend down and kiss her horribly deformed head, her hands. I press against her body and my desire to live returns. Even my blood pulses with renewed vigour. 'Mama, you will get well. I believe that, Mama. I've been acquitted! Love can conquer death. We will live, Mama. Can you hear me? We'll survive, we, maybe, maybe... we will even return. Forgive us, Mama, for not taking better care of you, for letting you starve yourself.' She's unconscious, but I believe, absolutely believe, that she will get well. I believe it, even though no one else does. I believe, even though the corpse brigade has arrived to take her away. But she's breathing.

I drag some more boards back to the barracks and light the stove. That same evening, Albertas and Platinskas are sentenced to three years in prison. Albertas's mother is now bedridden. He himself can still walk, but he sways like a drunken man. His mother had asked him for bread. 'But, Mama, where will I get it?' 'Steal it.' That night, together with Platinskas, he quietly left the barracks, crept into the bakery and took two loaves, but seeing so much bread at once, the two became giddy with hunger and couldn't wait until they got out of the bakery. Right then and there they began to gorge on the bread. At that moment, nothing could have stopped them, not the guards, not a trial, not prison. Each devoured an entire loaf and might even have died from so much food at once. But they wouldn't have budged for an earthquake. The patrol caught them eating. Each loaf weighed three kilos. While the charges were being drawn up and while they were being ushered into the lock-up, they crammed and crammed and crammed. Full stomachs, for once. But, as Albertas tells it, that feeling of fullness never came, even though his stomach couldn't have held one more bite. His mother died two days later, without having tasted a crumb.

Dzikas and one other Lithuanian were tried for counterfeiting vouchers. Instead of an extra ration of bread, they got three years.

Borisas Charašas was tried the following day – also for stealing boards. He was an incredibly handsome sixteen-year-old Jewish boy. He followed my example and admitted to stealing the boards, but the manoeuvre had lost its novelty for the tribunal and he was sentenced to a year.

Our barracks has turned into an infirmary. Scurvy has immobilized one person after another. Everyone has it. Anyone who claims to have survived the Arctic without succumbing to scurvy is lying. We all have it, though we're not all at the same stage. It begins with bleeding gums, which become swollen and bruised. Next the teeth start wobbling and fall out – breaking off painlessly at the root. Ulcers which remain painless for months appear on the legs. What's surprising is that no infection sets in – despite our filthy trousers, which stick to the open sores. Maybe our lice feed on the germs. Joints and muscles, usually those of the knees and calves, become painful. The only treatment is to keep moving, spend less time lying down; walking is essential. In the morning, the knee joints are stiff as lead – we can't stretch out our legs. Our solution is to slide off our pallets and begin to crawl. The pain is heart-wrenching. It's like having knives thrust into your calves. We crawl out of the barracks and head for work practically on all fours.

We are now hauling firewood to the office, the bakery and the steam bath, which will open soon. There are only five people in our brigade: Krikštanienė, Štarienė, Prapuolenienė, Nausėdienė and me. I urge them to get going, because I'm afraid of being late for school again.

I'm late every day. One after another, we crawl out of the
barracks, place the harness over our shoulders and creep
along, pulling the empty wooden sledge behind us. We
make our way, slowly, down the riverbank, crouched and
waddling, legs spread wide so our calves won't chafe. The
first kilometre is painful and difficult – our legs refuse to
bend at the knees. I can now understand my grandmother,
who used to complain that she couldn't walk because of
the pain in her legs. She moved very slowly and waddled
as she walked; you could tell that every step was an effort.
That's the way we're walking now, probably even worse.
Ahead of us is the mouth of the Lena River, which is
several kilometres wide and fettered in ice. Wherever the
wind has cleared the snow, the ice is as smooth as a mirror.
We hear booming, a sound like muted cannon going off.
That's the ice quaking. Huge fissures appear that reach
down its entire depth. We stop to rest, though we know
it will only make it harder to get our rigid, leaden legs to
bend again. We sit on the sledge. We are such tiny dots
against the imposing backdrop of the softly booming
Lena Delta. In the distance, we can see the shoreline of
Trofimovsk. We'd love to stretch our painful legs, which
are slowly giving out on us. But what if they seize up when
we stretch them out? Who will bring us back, at least as far
as the barracks? So we drag on. Staniškis and his brigade
overtake us. Like a man in a trance, Staniškis sways when
he walks – a stick dressed in the khaki green uniform of a
Lithuanian army officer. My hands feel numb inside my
gloves. I beat one against the other to the point of pain,

but nothing helps. If I suddenly need to pee – I've got a bladder infection – I'll just have to let it run down my leg. If I were to unbutton my trousers, I'd never get them done up again. We've crawled a distance of nine kilometres, but it feels more like 150. Our wooden shovels are too dull to slice through the deep, hard-packed snow. Here and there, we find some pieces of driftwood, a stick, a stump, a small log that has washed ashore. Štarienė stacks the wood in alternating layers, leaving a hollow space in the middle big enough to accommodate a crouching person. The side opening is covered with stumps. The stack is meant to look about two metres wide and high, when in fact it's probably less than one. We secure the sticks and stumps with ropes and hitch ourselves to the sledge. The runners do not slide easily, being made out of construction boards. Staniškis has an easier job hauling wood. Thanks to Vanagas, who like him comes from Panevėžys, he uses a sledge with steel-bottomed runners, the kind that is normally drawn by horses.

Our days of polar darkness appear to be getting lighter. The brightest moment of the day occurs during the milky period of twilight. But even that is a pleasure when you've been living in darkness for months on end. Hitched to fifteen or so sledges, Lithuanian and Finnish slaves move sluggishly, ponderously forward, step by step, like a funeral cortège that's several kilometres long. At the limits of our strength and bent close to the ground, we crawl practically on our hands and knees. The sledges do not want to slide and each step brings us closer to physical collapse. If I weren't actually attached to a harness, I'd probably fall. My hands and feet are frozen. The miserable scarf covering my face has turned hard as stone and is airtight from the condensation of my breath. I can't breathe. I can't see anything either – my eyelashes have frozen shut.

How foolish and pathetic we must appear against the splendour of the Arctic glacier. We are Ilya Repin's *burlaki*. But that painting of his, *Barge Haulers on the Volga*, is a hymn to human labour, unlike these fields of snow with their people who crawl like fleas in harness across the landscape. Trofimovsk seems beyond reach, even though it appears to be right here, within touching distance. That's an optical illusion, nature's teasing. It's always like that in the Arctic – the hours feel like years. An eternity. I could swear I've been pulling and pulling this damn load since birth, yet I haven't moved an inch.

Which of us wouldn't change places with Repin's *burlaki*? After a polar winter in Trofimovsk, pulling barges up the Volga would be like a walk along the Riviera. Someone suggested thinking about something else, or daydreaming, even reminiscing, as a way to speed up time while hauling firewood to Trofimovsk. But that is possible only for Repin's barge haulers on their riverside stroll, not for our cavalcade of emaciated nags. I'd often watched the nags in Kaunas, straining at their impossible loads, and would try to guess what they were thinking. Now I know what they were thinking: nothing. The mind is blank, movement is automatic. To stop is to fall and probably not get up again. I am slowly turning into a beast of burden, dying on the

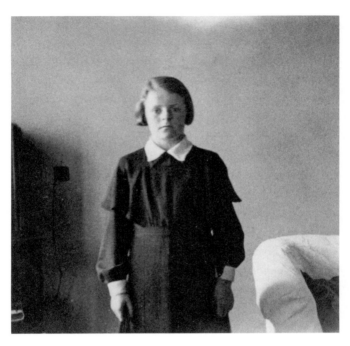
Dalia in her school uniform, 1938.

ice, harnessed to a sledge that's beyond my strength to pull. The horse's head is empty. On our return, we will eat our ration for the day – our chunk of bread – the magnet that draws us back to Trofimovsk. We fix the gaping holes in our hollow stack of driftwood to avoid arousing suspicion.

Then comes the hill: this is Golgotha, our Calvary. The tall, steep, crumbling riverbank. We stumble, we slip and slide, we dangle from our traces; the rope presses against our chests. Any minute now, the blood will spill out of our mouths – that's what it feels like. It was on this hill, as I remember, that I first felt a physical pain in my heart, as if someone had taken a pair of pliers to it. My young, immature heart protesting at the burden inflicted on it. I am light-headed, and now and then think I'm about to lose consciousness. I've become indifferent to the pile of cadavers in Trofimovsk, they leave me cold – unlike this hill of Golgotha. The first time I ever swore with curses so foul you'd wonder where I could have picked them up was on this damn hill. Each time we tug helplessly at our load, trying to get it up the riverbank, we are roused to insane rage, ready to tear to pieces all those who eat well without having to work. But – jaws clenched – somehow or other, we reach the summit. I watch Vanagas measure our load. Every time he cheats us, even if it's only by a single centimetre, we are ready to punch him in the face. Blind man that he is, he can't see that each stick has its tithe of blood, each one's collected with the last ounce of our strength.

Whenever my mother is sick, I buy bread for her, but I can't wait in line today, because the queue is so long and the school principal will scold me again. I return to the barracks, snatch up my books and inkwell, and slowly make my way to school on an empty stomach. The second period has already begun. I enter the classroom and before I've had a chance to remove my frozen scarf and scrape the ice off my face, I hear Guliayev asking me, 'Why are you always late?'

'I've just hauled in the wood. I come from work.'

'I can't put up with this any longer. Either you work or you attend school. If this continues, you'll have to drop out of school.'

I remain silent.

'Dalia, have you come straight from work?' asks Pticeva.

I say nothing.

'Have you had lunch?'

'No, I didn't get a chance. The queue was long and I was afraid of being late.'

I'm in pain with hunger. I've had nothing to eat for the second day in a row. I'm sitting at my desk. During break, I haven't the energy to get up and move closer to the stove. I might have pulled something inside me, lifting all that wood. I feel like an eighty-year-old with blocks of wood for legs. I sit resting my head on my hand. The sounds of the classroom recede. I'm back in secondary school, where I can see the dear faces of R., Z., and B. School, Lithuania, home, childhood… Did I really have a home once? And parents? Could there really have been people who took care of me, who worried that I might leave the house without my boots or show up at school without a sandwich? I smell the maddening scent of bread. Someone touches my hand. Pticeva is shoving something into my desk, something wrapped in newspaper – probably a piece of bread. I know she isn't hungry. Her father is a fisherman.

'Take it, I don't need it.'

I feel the pounding of blood in my head. I'm ashamed. A hand-out. From a classmate! My pride gets the better of me.

'Take it back. I have my own.'

But the look in her narrow eyes is deeply sympathetic; it pleads with me to accept the offering. How pathetic I must seem to everyone. I'd rather see hatred in someone's eyes than pity. I'd rather be struck, I'd rather starve for three more days, anything but that pitying glance in the eyes. That hurts more than hunger.

I rest my elbows on my desk. I feel my eyes fill with tears. I want to scream, but the sound catches in my throat. I realize my notebook is getting drenched; I see tears running down the side of my desk. I don't know why I'm crying. One more minute and I will lose all control. The scream that is caught in my throat will break free and I will sob out loud. The class is silent. We're all adults, although each of us is only fifteen years old. Pticeva presses softly against me. She understands everything.

There are only three of us left in class. Semionov is 150 kilometres out at sea, fishing. Kekonen has been caught stealing today and is being suspended from school by Guliayev. Yet Guliayev helps himself to all the bread, butter and sugar he can carry home. Eyes bulging angrily, he gave Kekonen an accusatory look and, grabbing him by the collar, flung him at the door.

'There will be no thieves in my classroom!'

Kekonen turned and answered, 'You… you, Principal, you're a thief yourself!' Then he ducked out of the door.

Tautvilas does not speak Russian, so they put him back in the sixth grade. That leaves just the three of us.

'I'm closing the seventh grade. It's not worth my while to pay teachers to teach just three students. You're free to go.'

My eyes grow dim from the shock. Guliayev's words have struck me like a blow between the eyes.

Professor Vilkaitis and Staniškis have died of dysentery. Vilkaitis had worked as a guard in Konstantinovka. Several days ago, Zigmas Steponavičius, a former student of Vilkaitis when they were both at the Academy of Agriculture, went from barracks to barracks pleading for a handful of rice for his professor. But how could anybody give him any, when they themselves had dysentery and no rice to spare? You can give only what you have, so the saying goes. Zigmas even asked Travkin for 200 grams of rice, but he wasn't about to give anything! Dysentery is the final stage of scurvy. The desire to eat does not disappear. The person with dysentery claims that he's tormented by hunger and is dying of starvation… The doctor has strictly forbidden those suffering from dysentery to eat. But they still get their usual ration, of somewhat whiter bread, dry it out and chew it. But no one with dysentery lasts very long. There is only one way to recover from dysentery and that is to eat a diet that is as rich in fat and nutrition as possible. I don't remember who it was and in which barracks, but someone did just that. Seeing that he was going to die anyway, because everyone, without exception, died of dysentery, he wanted to eat his fill before he died. Strictly speaking, this was just hunger out of habit, the hunger of hungers, since those suffering with dysentery don't feel hungry any more. So they brought him his ration of butter, 500 grams of sugar and some American pâté. He ate the butter and sugar together, next the tinned pâté and, finally, his bread ration for the day. Everyone stared ravenously at his every bite, expecting him to die. Instead a miracle occurred – the dysentery disappeared. He began to eat in earnest and somehow he recovered. The same thing happened with my brother and Grockis.

Abromaitis and Tamulevičius are carting corpses to the hill by sledge. The brigade of two shuttles non-stop between the barracks and the graveyard, ferrying dead bodies. Most of the bodies are naked, a few are wrapped in sheets. There is no way for the burials to keep pace with the arrivals. Bodies lie piled up like frozen logs. The Arctic foxes, which are also starving, gnaw on the cadavers. Every night, Misevičienė, a high-school principal's wife in Lithuania, goes to our little hill and pushes cadavers extracted by the foxes back into the pile.

Gamzienė has died. She was a beautiful forty-year-old Jewess in the seventh Jewish barracks. Her family were industrialists. Back in the Altai territory, we shared the same barracks. She was a warm and charming woman who adored her son, Nolia – a tall, slender, exceptionally bright eighteen-year-old. Every evening, we'd sit huddled together by the stove. In those days, we had not yet experienced hunger and were fed by the illusion of an early return home. Nolia would close his eyes and sing in a deep baritone.

Tamulevičius and his corpse brigade enter the seventh barracks to collect Gamzienė's body. Nolia is lying by his mother's side. He is sick too, and because he has not been able to get up his toes have succumbed to frostbite and gangrene has set in. Lice crawl across Gamzienė's face and chest, then cross over to her son and their neighbour on the right. Tamulevičius notices a chunk of bread the dying woman has hidden between the rags on her chest. It is also crawling with lice. Quick as a flash, Tamulevičius reaches out, snatches the bread, flicks off the lice and pops it into his mouth. Gamzienė's tattered clothes have frozen to the icy brick wall.

An average, torturous work day has ended. I'm sitting by the stove. As is usual by now, stolen boards crackle in the fire. So much for the tribunal. We steal because we have to – each of us, in turn – except that now we do it in pairs, in order to have someone to act as lookout. Nausėdienė is the only exception. She's the only one who doesn't steal: she can't, the entire essence of her being revolts in protest. She has never taken so much as a shred of clothing from the state. And she has stayed that way, even in the Arctic. At first, we were astonished, thought of her as a good omen in our midst. Then her integrity began to irritate. We were ready to tear the roof off Sventicki's house, whereas she would never even get upset. She explains, 'Believe me, I just can't.' So we leave her and her principles in peace, if for no other reason than that she is indeed a rare bird.

It's the first day of Christmas. We're out gathering firewood but haven't yet begun to forage on the Lena's far shore when it begins to snow with blizzard force. We can't very well return empty-handed so we keep going. By the time we decide to turn homewards, the trail has vanished. The fresh, powdery snow and the enormous snowdrifts make walking laborious. A nightmare. We're blown off our feet, we sway and fall into our traces. The wind pummels our sides, flips our sledge over, tears out our driftwood and flings it whistling and howling through the air. We lose our trail.

Then polar night descends. We can barely recognize each other; we've turned into sculptures of ice and snow. The snow is in our gloves, down our necks, inside our trousers. The Totoraitis girl gets frostbite on her toes – her felt boots are old and torn. Her rope goes slack. She can't pull any longer, she can hardly walk. We consider disentangling ourselves from the sledge and taking our chances separately rather than perishing together. Maybe, it being Christmas Eve, some of us will survive. But Krikštanienė – that wonderful woman, who is as strong as a man and calmly rational in every circumstance – tells us to wait. By pure luck, we reach Konstantinovka and, turning our faces into the wind, slog on in the direction of Trofimovsk. The blizzard topples us and our sledge several times, but we succeed in reaching the top of the hill – our Golgotha. Vanagas takes an approximate measure of our load with his eyes and orders us to tow it to the school. The last 200 metres are especially gruelling. Once there, we stop. Totally worn out, we take a few minutes to disentangle ourselves from our traces. All five of us, silently, without a word.

Vanagas has long since disappeared into his kennel. Whether we unload the wood here or somewhere else, who's to know? Let them prove what they want later. In the blink of an eye, the sledge is moving again. We're towing the whole lot to our barracks. Nausėdienė's conscience is probably squirming uncomfortably, but what the hell – she'll enjoy the heat from a hot stove as much as the rest of us on Christmas Day. We encounter supervisor Mavrin wrapped in furs. He probably thinks we're taking the load to the infirmary. Five minutes later, the empty sledge is on its side, the wood stowed indoors. The stove is hot. Three rubles in wages and our own firewood into the bargain.

Inside our ice-armoured barracks, I again trip over the bucket, which steams repulsively and reeks of urine.

We've all suffered frostbite. It shows in large, white patches on the face, which we rub with snow, and ulcers around the waist.

Krikštanis is eager to start chopping wood.

'Hey, Barniškienė, get your kid off the block. I've got wood to chop.'

Behind me stands the chopping block, but there's something white lying on top of it. I walk over and bend down to touch it. It's the small corpse of a child. So Barniškienė's little boy died today.

'I don't have anywhere to put him,' says the mother.

'Stick him under the bunk.'

For a moment, the white body of a child briefly appears before my eyes, then disappears. Albertas slides into the barracks. He has come to say goodbye, he shakes everyone's hand. I am sitting by the fire. He sits down next to me and lights a cigarette, then hands me some tobacco, which I also roll into a cigarette. We sit silently together.

'I'm glad, Dalia, to break free of this hell. The labour camp in Stolby can't be any worse. Really, it won't be worse than this. In any case, my mother's gone. I can endure three years. Then I'll return to life. And afterwards, Dalia, we will have a good life. I'll endure everything. I never thought the desire to live could be so intense.'

Then, leaning in close to me, he adds convincingly, 'We're young, we'll live. We will definitely survive.'

I crawl out of the barracks, but before going to work with the logs, for a moment I step onto the roof, which is level with the snow. The barracks lie deep beneath the snow. The weather is changeable. The surface snow is being whipped about by the wind, but there is no blizzard. The party of thirty or so prisoners is heading downhill towards the river. There are many Lithuanians among them. I see Dzikas, Riekus, several women, Borisas Charašas. Petrikas is herding them at gunpoint; he's also Lithuanian and has volunteered for this unpleasant job. I recognize the slender figure of Albertas in a thin, blue, lightweight coat. God, but this is insane – he's innocent. They'll never make it in this weather. It's like putting your hand into boiling water and thinking that you won't get burned. He turns around, waves. The wind picks up and starts whipping the snow about more furiously. Before long, the entire party disappears into the intensifying vortex of the storm. Not only does the faraway cliff of Stolby vanish from view along with the opposite shore of our river, but so does our small cemetery hill. Goodbye, and again goodbye. The blizzard howls, thunders and covers everything in sight. Then – everything goes into convulsions.

That night, I dream of Albertas. He is picking flowers in a meadow filled with magnificent blooms. Suddenly, his face appears in front of me. I see his eyes – beautiful, blue and melancholy. The wind ruffles his blond hair. 'It is finished,' he says, then shudders and closes his eyes. I sit up and scream. I get only a terrible howling in reply. Sky and earth clash. Our barracks shakes. Whirling like a dervish in the spaces between the ceiling boards, the snow descends in a vortex on the people huddled and shivering beneath their tatters. The polar elements sweep across the tundra, obliterating everything that is alive. The din outside merges into one deafening rumble of sound. The savage elements are clamouring for atonement.

The prisoners never reached Stolby. God, you terrible God, where are you? Where is your mercy? You are power-less in the face of such insane strength. You don't exist. You're a clay statue.

Gradually, the terrible howling dies down and, like a wounded beast, the blizzard expires.

The only ones to return are Borisas Charašas and Riekus. The prisoners had marched only five kilometres when the blizzard began. They hadn't even crossed the Lena to the opposite shore. They lost their sense of direc-tion and couldn't tell on which side of the river Stolby lay. They should have turned back, but they could no longer agree which side Trofimovsk was either. So they all went their separate ways, each one convinced that he alone had an accurate sense of direction. Borisas and Riekus almost missed our landmark pile of logs. But they did manage to crawl back to the barracks. Borisas suffered frostbite on his hand, which turned gangrenous and black. He now lies in the seventh barracks, his lifeless left hand cast uselessly to one side. His fifteen-year-old boyish face twitches with pain. He bites his lips, swallows tears. He refuses to give in, so with his remaining strength he launches into one operatic aria after another. Sometimes, the singing stops and then his screams are harrowing.

A gaunt young Jewess with astonishingly beautiful features snuggles next to him, sobbing soundlessly. In the darkness of the barracks his 'Laugh, Pagliaccio' takes on a macabre tone. Again silence. And then, 'God, oh, God,' Borisas screams. 'Why does it have to be my hand?

I've never caressed anyone with it yet.' And loses consciousness.

Riekus has frostbite damage to his feet, but maybe gangrene won't set in. No one else has returned alive and not a single dog sledge has run across their frozen remains. They have gone their separate ways and perished. On this side of the Trofimovsk tundra or somewhere among the labyrinthine channels of the Lena River. Or perhaps in the caves of Sardach, whose icy summits glisten in the sun. Before total polar night sets in, the remains of Petrikas and Dzikas are discovered accidentally by a Yakut on his dog sledge. He says he buried them. So he says. Goodbye, Albertas.

'We're young, we'll live, Dalia. I can feel it – we'll survive all this. We will definitely survive...' Goodbye, Albertas.

Borisas Charašas is in the infirmary. Each day, each hour is an exhausting confrontation with death, with the icy jaws of the North. At each step, the icebergs and the snows call out to us: 'Die, freeze, perish. You are our prey.' We have grown coarse. There is little that bothers us any longer. Corpses, typhus, scurvy – no big deal. There are no more people to be seen moving about in Trofimovsk, just naked corpses, frozen hard as stone, piling up on our little hill. When will it be our turn? We look at each other. Appalling as it is, we can tell who the next candidate for the hill will be from a tell-tale flickering in the eyes, which are enormous, the only feature left in an emaciated face.

Every day in the twilight hours of early dawn, three hours before Zagurski's wife opens the store, stooped creatures emerge from their barracks and inch towards the building. Walking skeletons – the only thing missing is a scythe. The cold is blistering. The snow sweeps across the surface of the tundra. We huddle together more tightly. Each of us aims to get as close as possible to the door. It's frigid. More Finns, Lithuanians, Jews arrive. A young Finn is standing in front of me, his chest bare. Nothing on him except a padded jacket. His eyes are blank, his face pale, jaundiced. He's telling me something, his lips move, but he makes no sound. He's offering to buy my day's ration of bread. The minutes and hours creep by slowly. There before me in the bread line, the young Finn crumples to the ground and dies with his eyes open. He's pulled off to the side. A debilitated but still relatively husky Lithuanian takes the ration card from the Finn's jacket pocket. That's an extra 300 grams of bread for him today. No one is in a rush to sell us food; the store opens half an hour late. People push and shove each other across the threshold. Those who are steadier on their feet push aside the rest, who fall and are stepped over.

The bread arrives. It is fresh, its aroma intoxicating. The man in front of me is a Lithuanian, from the country-side most likely. Lice crawl across his neck and down the back of his padded jacket. Slowly, solemnly. Then they cross over to me. I will probably get typhus. But I don't have the strength to back away from him – and someone is leaning against me. A queue has formed. Every day a queue – as exhausting as a day's work hauling firewood. Had I really been able to eat my fill in Lithuania? Why was

I such a picky eater? Will a day really come when I'll have as much bread as I like? I feel weak, my temples pound. I'm getting light-headed. I'm going to faint. I tighten my grip on our ration cards… Consciousness returns. I'm lying near the store. In the snow. There's snow in my mouth, in my ears, since I hadn't secured the earflaps. I stand up and get back in the queue. My turn comes late at night, my workday done. I see Krikštanis standing just outside the door devouring his bread. And his wife's.

Mum is up and about, holding on to the bunks for support. Her legs tremble and twitch. Krikštanis watches her with ravenous eyes. He can't seem to believe what he sees; he's like a child in the presence of an astonishing toy. However did she manage to get up? How is it that she can still crawl? his eyes seem to ask, indignant at such a stubborn refusal to give up the ghost. I'm feeling feverish, but I'm afraid to lie down. People who get sick and take to their pallets for a day or two, their legs seize up. Afterwards, they can't straighten them out. That's what happened to Jasinskienė. She came home from work one day with pains in her legs. The next day, she should have forced herself off her pallet. Little by little, the legs would have loosened up. Instead, she refused to go to work, said it was over for her and did not get up. Now she moans in pain. She screams every time her small daughter, Dalia, brushes against her legs. Some onions and a couple of raw potatoes, and the cramps in her legs caused by the scurvy would subside.

*

Borisas has been taken by sledge to Tiksi to have his hand amputated. The doctor doubts it can be saved, since it has been completely overtaken by gangrene. At each opportunity, Sventicki likes to remind people, '*Budete znat, chto znachit vorovat gosudarstvennoye imushchestvo. U nas tsena za dosku – ruka.*'– 'This is to remind you what it means to steal state property. Here the price of a board is a hand.' But when the supervisors run out of firewood and a blizzard prevents us from gathering it for them, they tell us to fetch some boards. They're afraid of freezing too, yet they live in log houses. That infuriates me and I go right on stealing boards, to Sventicki's great displeasure. Yet Sventicki has probably sent Borisas to his death. Whenever there is a blizzard, I don't even bother stealing from the depot but crawl right up to Sventicki's house and lift whatever wood is there. If he's chopped some boards, I drag them home; if there are logs, I take those too. We're no different from you, Sventicki; we like to sit by a warm stove as well when there's a blizzard raging outside. We're tired of shivering and dying like dogs from the cold and we know you always have a fire going, Mr Columbus of the North.

I really despise him. His stomach is full, his wife – the store manager. They aren't even interested in mere bread. They fill up on tinned American food and condensed milk, while our children starve to death. As soon as we stop to rest from hauling logs, he appears out of nowhere – a sneak with feline stealth – and orders us to get up. Our ration cards are distributed at the beginning of the month.

But if someone comes down with scurvy and can't walk or is just too weak to haul firewood from far away, he'll withhold that person's ration card at the store. He will not give the person any bread, thus forcing him to become a ward of the state, which entitles him to only half the usual ration. The snake has also introduced a mid-month validation date for ration cards, so that anyone who stops working by the fifteenth of the month gets his bread ration confiscated too. He's so 'generous' with the rations that people end up debilitated, bloated, and can barely walk. It's why they don't come to work. After all, truancy is a consequence of scurvy; a person will crawl to work for as long as he can. That's obvious to everyone. Sventicki seems to be the only one who doesn't catch on. Sitting behind his desk at the office with his double chin, his dog-pelt shirt and his knee-high winter boots, he feigns surprise at any suggestion that famine has come to Trofimovsk: 'Famine? What famine? There is no famine. The food you get is adequate and wholesome...' I go blind with rage when I hear that; I can barely keep myself from hurling the ink bottle at him or sinking my teeth into his neck. That schemer Judas Golovlyov is a pygmy compared to this bovine. After my trial, Sventicki has taken to greeting me pleasantly. Narrowing his repugnant little eyes into a squint, he says, '*Nu kak, podsudimaya, a? Ha, ha, ha. Eto vsyo radi tvoyego zhe blaga, chtob s maloletstva otuchit vorovat. Eto zhe sotsializm. Brat gosudarstvennoye nelzya.*' – 'So, how's the accused, eh? That was all for your benefit, you know, to discourage you from getting into the habit of stealing as a child. This is socialism, after all. Stealing state property is prohibited.' I glare back at him. And the amputation of Borisas's arm? Also in the interests of socialism? You are such a snake, Sventicki.

They've built a bathhouse. Everyone in the barracks is made to use it. Our turn arrives. We bring our clothes to a room where the garments are steamed and the lice rearranged – to improve the breed. The heat does not kill them, just warms them up a bit. Normally, men should bathe apart from women, but here the rules don't apply: we all bathe together. We can hardly feel embarrassed considering that, in the barracks, we see one another in every conceivable posture, responding to various calls of nature. Clothed or naked, you still feel like a louse. What appeal can a skeleton with protruding ribs and jaundiced skin have for anyone?

Krikštanienė says to Grockis, while bathing her husband, who has trouble standing, 'If you had any potatoes or bread to offer me, you might arouse my interest. As it is…'

It is, actually, a pleasure to undress and feel warm for the first time in six months, to wash away the dirt from a body that's been eroded by lice. Our breasts and armpits are spotted with pustules and scratched raw. There really is nothing here to arouse interest or shame.

After our steam bath, we retrieve our tatters, which are now infested with other people's lice. We can all recognize our own lice, and these – these are different! Noreikienė curses and swears that she has got Žukienė's lice with the little wings. Noreikienė flicks her lice to the ground and dresses. The results of the steam bath are dismal. Typhus comes to our barracks. The lice have obviously infected us. According to Kazlauskas, the bathhouse is a breeding ground for lice.

After her bath, Žukienė notices that her flour has been stolen. A few days earlier, she had traded a gold watch for eight kilos of flour. This morning she finds some of it gone. She wails with grief. Last night we were all awake on our pallets, when we heard someone rummaging in the dark, but since we couldn't see, we didn't know that person was helping himself to Žukienė's flour. A search by the light of some kindling revealed nothing. In the morning we left for the baths. Juozas was bedridden with his frostbitten feet, so he saw Grockis post his ten-year-old son to stand guard while he again helped himself to Žukienė's flour. Meanwhile, 'Sweet Genutė', the pious Štarienė, cleaned out the tins of food that her best friend, Prapuolenienė, had been saving.

Grockis was lying innocently on his pallet, but having filled up on what was essentially dough, he was moaning in pain. Now he's got diarrhoea and gets up every ten minutes to relieve himself in the pail, which has not been emptied for three days and reeks. No one suspects him. Prapuolenienė shows Štarienė her empty tins and complains loudly. She casts angry glances at Juozas and converses in hushed tones with her favourite, Genutė. Juozas can't be persuaded to speak up; he doesn't care that Prapuolenienė suspects him or that Žukienė wails in grief. He remains silent. Krikštanienė goes to open her tin, but finds it lying empty on the shelf. Krikštanienė weeps, while her husband – the 'emperor' – denies taking her tins. He claims that someone else has wolfed down their contents. Milė Noreikienė bets that it was none other than Krikštanis himself, says she heard him smacking his lips last night while lying beside her. She too finds her jug missing in the morning, the one from the Altai in which she had kept her milk, but which she and her boy, Daliukas, were now using as a chamber pot. Apparently, Krikštanis got the 'runs' last night. Since his own pots and jugs were already full, he went to use Noreikienė's but crushed the jug when he sat on it. Noreikienė searches for it by the light of her kindling and finds her jug in shards.

Milė Noreikienė's husband had been a civil servant at the Lithuanian consulate in Warsaw, and she his elegant and beautiful wife. She has lots of photographs from those times. These days she flirts with supervisor Mavrin. She used her connection to put her friend, Nausėdienė, in charge of the ration-card office. The two of them bunk together, like Prapuolenienė and her 'Sweet Genutė'. Mavrin is old at sixty, but Noreikienė tells me she will marry him, because it has always been a fantasy of hers to find a husband whose surname begins with 'M'. Whenever she has a date with Mavrin, she grooms herself conscientiously for lice and washes with the snow under the bunk. Then she comes to me with a lighted piece of kindling to ask whether her eyes are glowing. I tell her that she's glowing all over. She smiles radiantly.

'Daliukas,' she says to her son, 'if we ever meet Daddy again, don't tell him where I go. I'll bring you back some bread, maybe even some cocoa.'

The boy does not understand that his mother is going on a 'rendezvous', but he knows what 'bread' means and calls out in a deep baritone to his mother from under his tatters, 'Hurry!' Noreikienė slides out of the snow-covered door on her stomach and through the tunnel that has formed as a result of all the blizzards that have entombed our brick building. Daliukas never leaves his pallet or the rags that cover him. He is always cold, always famished. Juozas once told him to put a piece of bread under his pillow in the evening, said he'd heard that it would turn into a loaf overnight. Starving though he was, the little munchkin gathered up his willpower and saved a tiny chunk of bread from his day's ration, then placed it under his pillow. During the night, his mother found the bread unexpectedly and ate it.

Daliukas cried hysterically, thinking he'd been tricked by the older boy. Juozas, how can you tease a starving child? His suffering is as real as yours. His mother does not mistreat him, she shares everything with him. She always brings him something after one of her dates. When she broke off with Mavrin, she took up with the school principal, Guliayev, then the radio-station manager, then Grigoryev, Sventicki and others. But she's not a loose woman, she just enjoys flirting. I don't even know whether she ever became their mistress, although they probably expected her to. 'Flirtation is hard, Dalia,' Milė tells me.

'Smiling all the time, figuring out what to wear when you have no skirt, and the seat of your padded trousers is torn and scraps of cotton batting dangle from your bottom, which you are constantly covering with a scarf to hide the holes in the fabric, while the lice, which have been defrosting in the warm apartment, crawl up your backside. All you really want to do is press against a wall to crush them and scratch where it itches. Instead you have to smile, even though your stomach's growling. It's really tough, Dalia, flirting in the Arctic.'

Everyone likes Milė Noreikienė, because she's lively, funny and warm-hearted. She loves her friend Aldona Nausėdienė and calls her by the diminutive, Aldutė. During the long, eerie nights of polar darkness, when there's a furious blizzard howling outside, the two of them lie huddled together under their tattered covers, reminiscing. They talk about their university days in Lithuania, about the parties they attended, the letters each received from her first love, about travelling abroad. Both are thirty years old. Milė's eyes glow in the dark, and I can hear them whispering. They tell each other absolutely everything, down to the most intimate details. Spellbound, eyes fixed on the darkness, they talk without noticing their surroundings. They have moved to a place beyond the nightmare and for a while live completely inside their memories. I learn everything there is to know about them. It is uncomfortable listening to their shared intimacies.

We are all immersed in our memories. I think of all sorts of things from my past: home, school, Dad, friends, teachers, Palanga, the sea. Images of a happy childhood move frame by frame before my eyes. The only thing I can't think about is the theatre. I only have to recall the red velvet curtain, the orchestra, the first notes of *La traviata*, and my throat tightens and I can hardly breathe. It's like losing consciousness. I pull the tatters over my head and cry. 'That did not happen, it did not happen,' I tell myself over and over, unable to decide whether it was real, just a dream or my own hallucination. My imagination is impaired, my head feels concussed. No, I'm probably mistaken. It's a product of my imagination. It never happened.

But the hunger in my gut is too sharp. This terrible place – this prison, this fortress on the bleak, icebound tundra – is too real, too horrific; the sores on my shoulder from the harness to which I am hitched are too deep.

I'm afraid of thoughts that bite and sting. Images from the past can be more painful than a branding iron. They tear me apart. But they've also done me a favour. They've ignited a furious desire to live, to persevere, to engage in the struggle for life, even if what remains to be endured turns out to be a hundred times worse. I want to live, to live, to be alive, to return to life, damn it.

The girl I met at the campfire in Zayarsk lives in the barracks next door. Her name is Liuda and she's from Šiauliai. Both her brother, an army officer, and her mother, who worshipped Liuda and begged people to look after her, have just died. Liuda herself told me.

All of Liuda's friends are grown women. Černeckaitė was deported from Šiauliai with her lover. Now she lives with a Russian in Konstantinovka, where she feels neither hunger nor cold, and doesn't have to work either. Same thing with Paulauskienė, who moved in with the boat foreman. The teacher Saulevičienė took up with the Kazakh Tuminas, who is two metres wide. All the Lithuanians, especially the women, condemn them and call them 'whores'. In our barracks, it's 'Sweet Genutė' who is especially outraged by these women. Yet she herself fools around with the tractor driver. But what's there to be outraged about? Each does as she wishes. These women are only trying to survive. You can hardly call it lust, for it isn't about desire any more. Starvation put an end to that. Even if it were, what's so terrible about that? Life is short. This must be completely natural for some people; it lies in our nature to act in this way.

Baltrukonienė perished during the Christmas blizzard. She worked as a cleaning woman at the bakery and was probably the only one among us who wasn't starving. She was going to work. The bakery was only about five metres from her wooden barracks, but the insane, howling blizzard must have blown her right past it. During a snowstorm, you can't see it from the barracks. She never returned. Zagurski wanted to take her four-year-old boy, Jaunutis, but Stalauskienė wouldn't let him; she took the child herself. Baltrukonienė's body was not found.

*

One day, a mechanic is brought to the infirmary by dog sledge. He was found thirty kilometres from Trofimovsk, bound and lying on the ice. It seems that his wife had absconded by sledge with a prisoner. The husband had then jumped into a second sledge and given chase. The two teams of dogs began to race each another. Suddenly, the first sledge stopped. The wife and the prisoner waited until the second caught up, then they boarded it, tied up the husband and threw him out on the ice. He tried crawling but, gradually overcome by sleep, he began to freeze. Now one of his legs has to be amputated at the crotch. Our doctor, Griko, has come to borrow some iodine. Milė Noreikienė brought a bottle of it from Lithuania. The doctor also borrowed a couple of saws, including a carpenter's saw, and began to operate. No anaesthesia. The mechanic fainted several times, but Griko kept on sawing the leg, back and forth, like a log. She had no surgical equipment. The patient died before Griko finished amputating. You can never get Griko to come to the barracks. She's afraid of catching typhus. She won't go near an infected patient, instead treating each one from a distance.

When our mother was sick, Juozas went to fetch Griko, telling her that if she didn't come, he'd strangle her. That worked. Griko entered the barracks white as a sheet and for a moment was too terrified to move in our luxurious quarters. Shocked by the stench, she covered her face with a handkerchief and started muttering to herself. The thirteenth barracks, with all its dead and dying, must have made an unpleasant impression. My brother's eyes locked

onto hers and like a magnet drew her to the pallets. She
examined Mum by the blinding illumination of two pieces
of kindling and one lighted candle, which I had stolen
from the store. Diagnosis? 'Inflammation of the kidneys.'
What an idiot! Mum swelled up as a result of starvation.
Inflammation of the kidneys! I'd like to see you come down
with an inflammation like that. From every corner of the
barracks, the sick and the dying began to call for her, but,
obviously terrified, she started backing out of the room
towards the door. She wouldn't even stop at the pallet of
Atkočaitienė, who was lying near my mother. Which is just
as well: Atkočaitienė found her way to the afterlife without
Griko's help. Krikštanis, who was sitting by the stove with
Oldas Totoraitis and Kazlauskas, had been following her
every move. He laughed in her face and sent her out the
door with a hail of curses.

Frania Glushina was the doctor's assistant – a tall, slender girl from Belarus. She was about nineteen years old
with dark eyes and curly black hair. A girl of rare beauty.
Rarer still, she was very serious. And afraid of nothing.
She was in the constant presence of suffering, she saw
people dying of disease and starvation. Yet she could be
found everywhere, except at home, where she could have
been spending her time quietly playing cards with Griko
in a splendid apartment. Not a day passed that she didn't
enter our barracks. She knew everyone and they knew her.
She was the one ray of sunshine in our appalling morgue.
Griko demanded that patients come to see her in person,

sitting behind her desk, where she received them from three metres away. The sick had to crawl to the infirmary, often dying before they arrived – which made it easier for the morgue brigade. No need to tear the dead off their pallets and drag them out of the snowbound door by a rope around their feet.

Frania always visited the patients herself. She didn't let them get up, even if they wanted to. She was humane. A member of the Young Communist League, she was genuinely compassionate, and I could see that she'd even have risked her life to help these Lithuanians and Finns, who were foreign to her. I once lied when I told her I had dysentery and was voiding blood. I just wanted two days' rest from work. When she raised those magnificent black eyes that could bring a man to his knees, I saw in them the deepest kind of empathy.

'*Ty, Dalia, ochen stradayesh, naverno.*' – 'You must be suffering terribly, Dalia.'

For the first time I felt ashamed.

'I lied to you. I'm not bleeding.'

But she understood and, without another word, she lowered her eyes and signed a discharge form that gave me three days off work.

Mavrin, Zagurski, Sventicki, Griko, Travkin – all of them have stuffed their suitcases with goods bought from the Lithuanians for practically nothing. Griko bought a coat with a fox-fur collar from Mum. Now she has two coats, some fine dresses, thirty-five or so pairs of imported shoes, and more silk pyjamas and other luxury items than you can count. Our supervisors have the money to buy things. Sventicki sets the salary for our slave labour, which is delivered at the cost of our blood and our lives. His valuation: between one and three rubles per day. For three rubles, we haul logs all day. Two rubles is his assessment of a twenty-kilometre journey across snowdrifts with a sledge-load of firewood. Two rubles for the hill of Golgotha, two rubles for ulcers on our shoulders! Two rubles. What appalling exploitation, what contemptible mockery, what coldly calculated, deliberate murder. We sell our ration cards, when there is nothing else to sell, for the money to buy that pitiful allowance of bread they give us. Travkin could get some additional food for us from Yakutsk, but he doesn't. There is fish rotting in Konstantinovka, while we die of starvation, because supervisor Mavrin won't allow us to have it. He'd rather let it go off and dump it in the spring. Five hundred tonnes of fish were allowed to rot in the cellars of Sasylach and Bobrovsk rather than be used to feed us. That's how the Soviet Union really values its two-legged animals, which for some reason it continues to call human – in order, I suppose, to appropriate the few remaining possessions the Lithuanians had not traded for potatoes in Altai. Our supervisors load up on luxuries, while the pile of corpses keeps on growing – a monument to the Soviet state.

In this gallery of murderers, you alone, Frania, are splendidly noble. If I were a sculptor, I'd carve a statue of a woman leaning into the blizzard, carrying medicines under her fur jacket to our catacombs of disease and death. When, later in life, I read about the Russian mythical figure Danko, who led his people to the promised land bearing his own torn-out heart before them like a flag, it was you I saw.

I am standing in the bread queue. Supervisor Mavrin, his wife and his maid help themselves to fruit compote, tinned milk, powdered eggs and even oranges to ward off scurvy, without having to stand in a queue. Zagurski's wife, who is the store assistant and attending to a customer, complains that she's lost her appetite. Mavrin's wife suggests that Mrs Zagurski try a rice casserole with raisins and dried apricots. We stand there muzzled in ice, gawking like sheep – no appetite, imagine that. I absolutely cannot comprehend the fact that our overseers in Trofimovsk live comfortably in warm, two-room apartments in log houses, which we built for them with our own hands, that they have candles, that their apartments have light, that they can eat whatever they want. I thought that in wartime everyone was supposed to bear the burden equally, but these people don't feel the war at all. After it's over, they'll probably boast of the hardships they faced, their struggles in a distant land beyond the front lines and their personal endurance. They will describe how they inspired the masses to contend with the polar elements for the glory of the fatherland. They will be decorated, and the pit filled with Lithuanian and Finnish corpses will be regarded as a testament to their efforts.

Oldas is standing at the counter, picking up bread for the Totoraitis family. He hands his ration cards to Zagurski, who cuts out the appropriate coupons with his scissors and instructs his wife to measure out a double ration in a fraction of a second. Oldas then retrieves these coupons from the counter. Zagurski thinks he has placed them in the box. Today, the Totoraitis family will eat a double serving of bread. Oldas smiles at me. He's a decent man, good to his family and his mother. Now it's my coupons that are being clipped. Meanwhile, the store assistant is weighing the day's ration of bread for Markevičienė, who – in a single sweep of her hand – gathers up not only her own ration but also the small, leftover heel of the loaf, perhaps fifty grams' worth. Zagurski's eyes pop, the veins on his forehead bulge, he grabs a tin of food and whacks Markevičienė in the face with it. Blood spurts from the bridge of her nose and pours down her face. She crumples to the floor and crawls out of the store.

'These Lithuanians – they're cattle. You just can't treat them any other way.'

He's right, we are cattle: starving, dying cattle. We had just arrived in Trofimovsk when the tubercular Genė Markevičienė, with whom we shared the painfully cramped train journey, lost her infant son, her husband and three of her daughters. She buried the last one yesterday. And today Zagurski does this to her. He thinks he's lord of the store. The masses think he's God. We frequently debate the question: is Zagurski's stomach always full? We know he is the food lord, but we can no longer imagine how someone can be full, sated to the point that they don't want to eat any more. This is incomprehensible to an imagination stunted by famine. I wonder, Zagurski, whether you'd have dared to raise your hand against Markevičienė two years ago. I wonder if you'll be tried for it. If for nothing else, you should go to jail for this. But today, as God is my witness, Zagurski mocks and humiliates us. When he looks at us, all he sees are slaves, tottering and famished, barely able to move, debilitated by scurvy and starvation. At every opportunity, he lets us know that we occupy a lower rung of humanity, that we're the serfs. You're filthy and uncultured, your barracks are too squalid to set foot in. I never thought that Lithuanians liked living in apartments infested with lice and covered in shit.

'Is this the way you lived in Lithuania?' he asks.

Turning my back to him, I grab hold of a shelf to steady myself — I can feel my legs shaking. You stupid pig. Go ahead and jeer. It is easy to scorn a people on their knees.

Meanwhile, the Totoraitis family is eating a double ration of bread. Their daughter Birutė has dysentery, the mother has scurvy and can't get off her pallet. Her ten-year-old boy has no clothes though he's a lively adolescent. The eldest boy lives separately in a different barracks. His mother dotes on him.

Birutė, a bright and articulate twenty-year-old, was at university studying Humanities. An NKVD officer, a Tatar who boarded with the family, fell in love with her. When he learned that Birutė had been deported from Vilnius and that she was already on the convoy of trains, he ran after her, but it was already too late. On 14 June, he shot himself in the empty Totoraitis apartment. He left a suicide note: 'I die of injustice.'

Every fifteen minutes, Birutė climbs down, half naked, from her bunk and positions herself on the sanitary pail. Her once golden hair is grey and dishevelled, her naked chest gaunt. Her eyes are dreadful, mere holes in a faceless skull. She can't seem to get up from the bucket.

Krikštanis watches her struggle and says, 'If the Tatar saw her chest now, he wouldn't shoot himself but try to stop her diarrhoea, which is, technically, impossible to do. She's young but she will die soon.'

I'm disgusted. Why is Krikštanis prattling on about other people dying? He should take a good look at himself. He's an appalling sight too. I once found him collapsed on the ground with his trousers unbuttoned. I could barely get him back on his feet.

We've bartered Dad's jacket for three kilos of flour. Every day we make a soup from two tablespoons of flour boiled in water. Juozas can't get over the fact that we never prepared this 'dish' in Lithuania. If he survives, he says, he's going to have it often when he gets home. Every evening, we engage in endless conversations about food. Each of us describes our favourite foods, our favourite recipes. The topic is inexhaustible, constant. Some people find it comforting, but not me. I can see the food, all those tinned edibles, and my mouth waters, I feel weak. Everything irritates me. There's no way to escape the talk of food, it seeps into one's consciousness. I remember, back home in Kaunas, I once collected a bag of bread crusts that I hadn't eaten and didn't know what to do with, so I dumped them over an embankment on Perkūnas Boulevard. Those crusts now haunt my dreams and waking hours – their revenge for having been tossed out. I remember scenes at the dinner table, I remember my parents pleading with me to eat. On one occasion, Juozas and I were having crêpes with jam at the milk bar in Kaunas. We ate half of them and couldn't manage another bite, so we waited till the waitress left the room and went running out of the snack bar. We actually thought that someone would chase after us for not finishing our food. A believer in Alexei Suvorin's theories on the benefits of fasting, our Dad occasionally used to fast. When Kazlauskas heard about this, he raised his eyebrows and cursed to high heaven the wickedness of some people – imagine starving yourself in the face of plenty.

Twenty Finns – men who could still walk after a fashion – began to fish along the coast in return for food and they recovered their strength. So a second group of men left to try their luck. But a Yakut on dog sledge reported finding them frozen to death some thirty kilometres outside Trofimovsk. Their bodies were found lying next to one of the yurts, which the Yakuts build between thirty and forty kilometres apart for their own use and for that of other mushers in need of shelter. Unable to make headway in a blizzard that had overtaken them or to find the yurt that they knew was somewhere nearby, the fishermen dropped into the snow and fell asleep for good. Because of the blizzard, they couldn't see that deliverance was just an arm's length away. There had been several Lithuanians among them, but I never learned their names. If they'd stayed, they would probably have starved to death anyway, so maybe it was for the best that they died in their sleep. We had to wait until spring to bury them.

Entombed in Trofimovsk, time moved silently, oppressively, like a nightmare. The long polar night had indeed become an immense and terrifying grave. Fewer and fewer people crawled out of their barracks. Abromaitis's brigade appeared more and more often, fully loaded with corpses. The silence in all the barracks was now absolute. Death and disease ruled. The only ones who left our catacombs of ice daily were Krikštanis and myself. No one spoke any more, not even about food. The end was in sight. We would be moving to our small hill soon, that mounting pile of bodies which, like some sort of Eiffel Tower, was visible from our barracks.

Then the silence ended. The first blasts of the blizzard exploded like bombshells. Our barracks, fragile as matchboxes, shuddered. The worst, the wildest and the longest blizzard of the winter arrived to announce the rising of the sun. Separation between earth and sky, day and night, reality and dream disappeared. Complete upheaval.

Trofimovsk, that dot on the polar tundra, was plunged into a total nightmare.

When did the blizzard begin? When would it end? It feels like a lifetime since we've had any contact with the outside world. We've been buried alive. Twelve days straight. Even if the blizzard were to stop, we wouldn't be able to crawl out, because the long, tube-like passage we dug with our hands to the outside has been plugged solid. The door, which the wind ripped off its hinges, has been tossed under the bunks. It never closed anyway, it was coated with ice. Totoraitis is using it as a bed. There is a mountain of snow in the middle of the room, which the storm blew in through the hole we had excavated to the outside. But this is good. It keeps out the whirlwind. The blizzard has buried our brick barracks; its flat roof is level with the snow outside. There are gaps between the ceiling boards, which clatter softly in the wind. The powdery snow falls on our heads and pallets.

We have pulled up the floor, shaved wood from the beams that support the ceiling and chopped up the benches, as well as the boards that separate one family's bunks from another, for firewood. There is no reason to get up, nor does anyone have the strength. For the last five days, ever since someone threw three small loaves of black bread down the stovepipe, no one has had anything to eat. That was the day the insane howling diminished slightly and the shaking let up. But who had the will to get up and divide the bread that had reached us with such effort? I saw Krikštanienė getting off her bed of snow and ice. So I too put on my padded jacket. Though the sick and dying didn't need bread, they got their share anyway. Krikštanienė and I would never wrong the dying. She is an honest woman with incredible stamina. The devil has not yet devised the circumstances that could defeat her. She'll survive, I can see that, because survival is what she wants and she is making a superhuman effort to ensure it. That day, death by starvation had been pushed back by a few days. Suvorin was mistaken in his theories of fasting – in our experience, those who were already weak lived just five days without food. We burned the last of the floorboards and melted the snow in the empty tins, where it mixed with the excrement of those suffering from diarrhoea. We poured off the waste floating on the surface and offered the sick a final drink. Thirst was a constant torment. Thanks to the blizzard, we now have clean snow in the room, which we can scoop from our rags and suck on. We lie squeezed together for warmth. The barracks are completely dark. We've covered ourselves with everything we own, plus a snow blanket on top. It does provide warmth. The snow is everywhere – our pillows, our hair. You stick your head out, take a deep breath, slip under the covers again and breathe out. Feels warm. The snow on your hair melts, then turns to ice. A winter hat. Silence. Darkness... The only thing visible is the snow.

So here we are – creatures who once thought of them-selves as human, who laughed, flirted, called friends and invited them to visit, who planned summer holidays after exhausting winters of work in the city, who fumed because the tailor had botched an order or because a two-room apartment seemed small. All are silent. But then they are no longer here. The people they used to be have long gone. They died on 14 June. All that's left in the thirteenth barracks are the dead and the nearly dead. Only three categories of people remain: the corpses, the soon-to-be corpses and the dying who might survive. These survivors will bear witness to the horrific trials they have undergone. But by then each will have become someone else.

The brick walls shudder. One after another, the boards that the wind dislodged from the ceiling take off into the air, leaving ever wider gaps. As a result, the blizzard is now swirling inside with us. Our iron drum, the stove, has taken to bouncing up and down and produces a constant shrieking. Like a people condemned, we are silent, breathing our last beneath the covers. We are silent because we haven't the strength to speak; nor is there anything left to say, or anyone to hear us over the howling of the wind. We have lost hope. All is pointless. The last chapter in the human comedy. I am terrified of death. The hill of corpses on this land of permafrost and tundra terrifies me. Even a midsummer death means lying deep inside the tundra encased in ice. Never to decay because it will always be too cold. But I want warmth. I'm beginning to get used to hunger; I feel it less, I've got it tamed. A mental picture of bread no longer stirs the appetite. Just warmth, that's all I want. The blizzard, apparently, is never going to end. *Comedia finita est*, that's my last conscious thought. Then everything merges into a single dream, a single nightmare, a howling monotone: the senses lose their boundaries; this life and the next have become indistinguishable.

Silence. Wait… I can't resist. I stick my head out again. Yes, silence. Surely not! I listen intently – and, yes, I hear the rhythmic sound of shovelling. It's getting closer. The blizzard has stopped! Is it possible? I'm afraid to believe it, lest with a single bang the ghastly howling returns, and earth and sky conjoin again. If the nightmare comes back, we'll all lose our minds. Someone slides in on his stomach through a hole in the snow.

'Anyone here alive?'

Silence.

'People, speak up, say something.'

I lift my head and, with the last of my strength, sit up.

'Yes, yes… a-alive… w-we…' I can hear myself stuttering, my voice gone. My legs are trembling, I can't hold up my head, I'm weak, and tears are pouring down my face.

During the blizzard, we lost the whole family's ration cards. Death by starvation is staring us in the face.

A brigade of Cossacks from Astrakhan, supervised by Saulevičienė's husband, Tuminas, has been hacking a mass grave on the hill for three straight days. The work is hard. The pickaxes are constantly losing their edge because of the ice and gravel. The Cossacks curse obscenely in frustration. The factory management had received word that a sanitation commission was flying in. Time to clean up the evidence of its administrative incompetence. The pit is substantial – twenty metres by fifteen, and two deep. The Cossacks work rapidly. If they succeed in stuffing the tower of rigid cadavers into the pit on schedule, they will be paid thirty rubles for each day of work. A lot of money. Easier to stuff a grave with corpses than haul timber. Finally, the pit is finished. The corpses are hurled whistling into the pit, their arms splayed repugnantly. Their hands, legs and emaciated bodies glow in the darkness. Extremities have been gnawed by starving foxes, noses chewed off. The cadavers are frozen solid; when they fall, they clatter like sticks. Some land in an upright position, propped against a pile of other cadavers. The pianist A. stands naked, leaning against a naked pair of legs. Klingmanienė's stomach has been chewed open, the frozen intestines visible but intact, apparently unappetizing even to Arctic foxes. Her arms are splayed and the whites of her eyes glow in the moonlight. Suddenly, the Cossacks stop tossing corpses into the pit. There is not going to be room for all of them. The frozen cadavers are stiff and do not fall neatly into the grave in horizontal layers. So the Cossacks begin to bundle them with cord. With considerable dexterity, they arrange the naked dead side by side at the waist, commenting cynically as they work. The last chunks of ice and frozen earth will then cover what's left of these people, so varied in their backgrounds, their nationalities and professions. I am struck by the incongruity of it all. Three hundred people who had once been strangers to each other. Each had had plans for the future. Each had worked, built and created. How solicitously fate now gathered them together and buried them in one grave, bound like siblings for ever!

The gross national product for 1942: bundled and stacked. For successful completion of the project, Tuminas is rewarded with Mavrin's gratitude.

The sun appears for only five minutes. But each day more and more of the sun peeks over the horizon and shines for a slightly longer time – five, eight, ten, twelve minutes. It illuminates silent Trofimovsk, huddled against the vast glaciers of the Lena estuary, then sinks again into darkness. Not many of the poor unfortunates get to see it. No ray of sunlight can penetrate a structure buried up to the roof in snow.

We get home from work, we sit at the stove. I have the place of honour there: beside the open fire. No one dares to deny me that spot, since it was I who stole the wood that's burning inside. The fire feels good against my body, though my blotchy, frostbitten face hurts. Across from me sits the skeletal figure of Adolis Ašmantas, hugging the warm stovepipe. His stepmother and his three stepbrothers and stepsisters have died; he's the only one left. But his bladder has been damaged and he smells of urine. Especially when the fire takes the chill off his clothes. The stench – you want to run out of the room. His father was a locomotive engineer in Šiauliai. No one can understand why the family was deported. Then again, there were many like them: deported for reasons unknown. Adolis sits at the stove like a statue. Occasionally, he lets go of the stovepipe in order to brush lice from his clothes, which then drop in a sizzle onto the hot iron drum. Adolis laughs with satisfaction. The boy looks pitiful. Nausėdienė doesn't talk much. I respect her enormously. During the whole horrid time of our deportation, I never once heard her complain. She has managed to rise above our situation. Looking at her lovely, fragile, diminutive figure, you'd never guess she has so much inner strength. She's proud to a fault. Those who don't know her well think she feels superior to the rest of us. But she's always had it harder than the others: she has no possessions left, she doesn't have anything to wear. She suffered more than some when it came to starvation, but no one has ever known how to bear their pain as quietly and with as much dignity as she does. I think she has a beautiful face, there's something spiritual about it. It is the face of someone who has obviously suffered but who also knows how to endure suffering. She remains untouched by the petty animosities and hostilities surrounding her. She never moralizes, never preaches. Not even when Krikštanis denounced her to his supervisor for having worked in the Lithuanian intelligence service for five years. She never reproached him for it. He was just envious, thinking that she had worked in the Bureau of Records, when in truth she had worked only as an English translator in the Bureau's printing office.

I find myself wanting to be like her. I want my fight for survival to be like hers: quiet, dignified, untainted by trivia, never petty or mean-spirited. I will try to be like that. I want her to respect me. I know I can do it. I just have to be on my guard and work conscientiously at improving myself.

*

In crawl two creatures. Two men.

'Well, congratulations to the conquerors of the Arctic!' The mocking tone of a vigorous voice travels the length of our barracks.

A candle is lit. For a minute, the two men stand there, obviously shocked by the wretched sight. Both are covered head-to-toe in fur. They ask after those who are sick.

'Everyone is sick.'

'In that case, we will examine everyone,' answer the men. 'Boy, over here, hold the candle while we make the rounds.'

I'm in trousers and the padded 'hundred-thread' jacket – they take me for a boy. We move slowly from one pallet to the next. They ask me about everything, they want to be told everything. They don't question the patients much, but they do look at everyone's legs, lifting their covers to see what stage of scurvy they're dealing with, then shine a light into each face. Everybody looks the same: horribly sunken eyes, ulcerous legs that have turned black and can't be straightened out, swollen joints at the knees and throughout the body. Deformities of the limbs, protruding ribs.

The men get ready to leave.

'Don't lose hope. We've come to remedy the situation.'

They leave me what's left of the candle. A godsend. 'Boy…'

That was the Jewish doctor, Samodurov, who had a club foot. The next day someone shovelled out the entrance, making it large enough to exit upright if you stooped a little, and removed the snow that had been polluted by human waste. The gesture moved some of us to tears. When we returned from work hauling logs, we were told that Stepanovienė had come earlier in the day and made a list of the sick, even taken their temperatures. That evening we were completely stunned when she brought a small lantern made from a tin can and hung it from the ceiling. We can now see each other's silhouettes in the dark and won't be bumping into each other or stepping into the chamber pots. The lantern flickers and smokes terribly, and the snow above the candle melts and drips from the ceiling. But we can't stop looking at it. The chandelier in our dining room was pitiful compared to this tin of light. The important thing is that someone is taking care of us. We must be optimists by nature; we keep believing that things will improve. This time we are not mistaken. The next day the sickest patients are removed. The ones with scurvy are taken to one infirmary, the ones with typhus to another. The former are settled into a barracks that had been emptied only the day before of its surviving inhabitants, who were relocated to other quarters. The worst of the muck has been removed and both barracks have been disinfected. This is only a drop in the ocean, though. There isn't room in them to accommodate all of even the weakest patients.

Stepanovienė is a Jewess from Alytus, the wife of a doctor. She was expected to take Stefanija Jasinskienė, who has begun passing blood, to the infirmary. But Stepanovienė demanded that Jasinskienė hand over her daughter's ration

Laptev Sea

Tumat

Trofimovsk

Stolby

Bobrovsk

RUSSIA

Lena

Tiksi

The Lena River Delta.

card in exchange. Jasinskienė refused, saying she'd rather die than give Stepanovienė Dalia's card. So Stepanovienė took Birutė's card instead. And Birutė got to go to the hospital. But Birutė won't be coming back. That's obvious. Her diarrhoea is too severe, her bowels too far gone. Vincė Daunorienė's diarrhoea is even worse, but she too, as a matter of principle, refused to give Stepanovienė her card and stayed behind with Grockis and Jasinskienė to linger between life and death.

In addition, Liuda, that pretty girl from Šiauliai, came to our barracks and gave each of us fifty grams of sprouted peas. Even those who weren't sick received peas. That's become a daily routine. Those with scurvy are also getting pills. Each day more and more people are transferred to the infirmary. Except for Jasinskienė. Her condition does not improve, despite the pills and a double ration of pea sprouts. We tell Jasinskienė to stand up, try to convince her that standing will take some of the stiffness out of her legs. But she doesn't want to. The slightest touch and her screams are harrowing. The pain must be terrible, so we leave her alone.

We each receive a kilo of salted wild onions and a larger than usual serving of barley. Our situation improves daily and the sick begin to regain their health.

Birutė returns from the hospital and Vincė recovers. Dr Samodurov orders a large box of pills for Jasinskienė and her legs loosen up. They are no longer painful to the touch.

The day comes when Jasinskienė asks to be lifted from the pallet and set on the floor. We wrap her legs in rags, lift her down and plant her on her feet. She stands, legs spread apart for balance. We are afraid to let go – her legs seem so wooden. But we do. Miraculously, she remains standing. The sick, the healthy – everyone's watching her and smiling. Jasinskienė is smiling too, shyly at first, as if she were committing some crime. But her legs continue to hold, though she herself is trembling. She tries taking a step forward – but falls. We catch her before she hits the ground and lay her back on the pallet. She embraces her daughter, kisses her, and keeps reaching for her own legs, as though she'd just been made a present of them.

One more human being rejoins the living.

Praise and honour to the Jewish doctor, for he has earned them. He saved many of us from death. If it were not for him, I doubt whether any of us would have survived.

The Yakuts get paid in food for the fish they catch and are now bartering their food with us for goods. That has freed most of us from dependence on rations. The Yakuts come to us with offers of flour, barley, butter and sugar in exchange for men's suits, watches. Even though we have few things left, we manage to find something to trade. We even have pots on our stove now. Famine is a thing of the past. There is just hunger.

The sun shines, but without warmth. A plane arrives and out steps Borisas Charašas in the company of an official. Borisas's empty sleeve flutters in the wind. There are greetings. Borisas shakes hands with Mavrin, who smiles and says something to him. With his divinely beautiful face, Borisas smiles back. I assume this is all a bit of theatre, that at any minute Borisas will punch Sventicki in the face with his one good hand, and when Sventicki reels from the shock, he will understand what he has done to Borisas. But no. Borisas and the official are now chatting with Sventicki. I'm disgusted. I turn around and run back across the tundra, sinking into the snow as I head in the direction of our settlement. Could Borisas be right? Could Sventicki? No, no, a hundred times no. I am not mistaken. We are not cattle, we're people, we're just treated like cattle – killed, abused, taunted, buried alive. We're the ones who are in the right. Nor must we ever forget it. We must remember our grievances; justice is on our side. They are the criminals. I no longer find Borisas attractive. He's just a repugnant little bootlicker, a person with no self-respect. Someone who grovels before the enemy when he's got truth and justice on his side is pathetic, contemptible.

I'll take human decency and spiritual beauty over good looks any time. A kind and caring person will always be beautiful, whereas a face like Apollo's but without the spiritual qualities turns me off. Perhaps it's instinctual, this understanding of beauty. As far as I'm concerned, Borisas Charašas is not a handsome youth, he's pathetic. Samodurov, who is generally agreed to be grotesque because of his abnormally large and misshapen body, is beautiful to me because he is compassionate.

*

More and more people are up and about. Grockis has recovered. Each day he delivers water to the canteen which has been set up by Travkin on Dr Samodurov's orders. They've even found the funds for it. My mother queues up at the canteen daily and for lunch she brings back pea soup in an earthenware cup. Hitched to a sledge, Grockis pulls a barrel of water all by himself. I can't believe his strength. Turns out that the Finnish cook is secretly feeding him. But Grockis denies it. Marytė, who also works in the kitchen, says that the first day there he ate fifteen servings of thick pea soup, then doubled over on the kitchen floor in pain. As soon as the pain subsided, he asked for more. Digrevičienė is also delivering water by sledge. She's a tall, strong woman. A hermaphrodite, according to the Russians. She's very masculine and walks like a sailor, swaying from side to side, with her hands in her pockets and her hat perched on the back of her head. Coarse too! Prapuolenienė is back on her feet, as are Stefanija Jasinskienė and Juozas, who want to join our wood-hauling brigade again. Krikštanienė doesn't like to admit men into her brigade because, she says, they're weaker than children. Grigas, Mikas and Juozas all sway in the wind when they walk. Putting them to work seems out of the question. Women are more resilient to starvation. But Krikštanienė did not admit Noreikienė into her brigade so, along with a few other malingerers, Noreikienė organized her own team. Little by little, her brigade began to attract the ones who could only crawl, the living dead, who by some oversight had neglected to die. Her team of cadavers and malingerers has grown to twenty in number, none of whom work much, including their brigade leader, Milė Noreikienė. Instead she spends her time flirting with Grigoryev and Sventicki. She and her brigade earn more than we do.

Everyone still alive has been put to work hauling logs again. There is no longer any need to haul firewood. The company has acquired two horses that can carry as much as ten brigades of emaciated two-legged nags. Now we are shovelling the snow from the logs we stacked in the autumn. Along the riverfront, buried deep under the snow, lie several hundred thousand logs. They have to be retrieved and brought to the shore before the ice begins to melt and the Lena pushes them out to sea. We wait hopefully for summer, believing that our Arctic expedition must end then. We're convinced that the first convoy out will take us somewhere else, at least to a place of trees and grass instead of glacier and naked tundra. Somewhere we could chew grass, if we had to, and have wood to burn. Grockis says that if the convoy fails to transport us out of here, we should grab hold of the barges and steamers and leave by force if necessary.

We will never survive a second winter here – that is the absolute conviction of all the exiles in Trofimovsk. But when we look at the stacks of logs, from which we have already cleared two metres of snow, and at the hundreds of thousands of them still lining the shore from here to Konstantinovka… The logs have obviously been brought in for construction purposes. Which means the company plans to expand. We're the labour force, after all. Why would they let us go when they specifically brought us here to '*osvoyit Sever*' – 'settle the North' – as Sventicki would say. But the thought of another winter, another long polar night, is so terrifying and absurd that I too am inclined to believe that we will not be wintering here again.

One after another, the brigades make their way up the icy hill of Golgotha. A string of sledges with no end in sight. Two Cossack brigades are hacking at rafts that have been trapped in ice since the autumn. Hauling logs feels easier now – the rope does not dig into the flesh as painfully as before, because our shoulders have developed calluses and the scar tissue has become less sensitive with time. Yet by the end of a fourteen-hour day, my shoulder has been rubbed raw again. Like Repin's barge haulers, I sling the rope across my chest and keep it pressed tightly there with my hands. But that creates different problems. Then I feel a crushing weight on my heart, I feel my temples throb, the blood vessels in my neck bulge and pound, and pound and pound. I get light-headed, I pant like a dog. Days, weeks, months become indistinguishable. Try as I might to recall some other memory, I can't. There is just Golgotha, with its logs, snow swirling underfoot, and rope, more rope and nothing but rope… And just a single thought, a single desire: to get this one log up the hill. Just to get it up. Just this one, this log only, just this one.

Oh, Golgotha! The Golgotha of my youth, the spring of my life. I see that, except for brief interludes, I will have to live with you for the rest of my days. You were the first to shape my character. If I'm tenacious, I have you to thank. It was here that I learned to suffer patiently, to inch painfully towards the summit. Then, upon reaching it, to experience the pleasure of achievement and a growing faith in my own powers. Golgotha, my cruel and unforgiving teacher. The first to teach me about life, how to fight and how to overcome. How to clench your jaw and suffer, without screaming or moaning about it. It is here, hitched to a rope, harnessed to an impossible load, bent double from the strain or crawling on all fours up the side of your hill, Golgotha, that I learned how to hate. And I thirsted for revenge against everyone and everything that demeans and brutalizes other human beings.

Working on a stack of logs next to ours is a four-man brigade of prisoners. They are dressed for the winter. They all wear padded trousers and jackets and warm footwear. Fur gloves too. Like the Cossacks, they gird themselves with the red *kushak* – a ten-metre strip of wide red cloth which they wind around their waists. I noticed that all the dockworkers on the Lena River wear such *kushaks*. They use them as a precaution against rupture. The prisoners' faces are red and robust; they eat well. The eight of us can't keep up with the four of them. One of them, an especially nimble worker, shovels the snow from one part of the stack. Two others lift the log out of the pit with their hands and send it, like a bolt of lightning, flying onto the sledge. The fourth man steadies the log, then, with just the ends of the logs resting on the sledge, two of them begin to pull. Another second and they're running along an icy path for about 500 metres and then straight up the riverbank. Meanwhile, the eight of us are still struggling to lift one log out of the pit.

The prisoners overtake us near the hill; it's their second run.

'You're not eating enough porridge, girls!' they shout.

One of them is very handsome, he reminds me of Albertas. Blond hair, soft, deep-blue eyes. The gracefulness and ease of his movements put him in a different class from the others. I learn that he isn't a prisoner but a Finn named Reino. He never gets into any shoving matches, and whenever any of the others use filthy language, he just watches sadly. He seems such a wholesome young man. I really like him! Once he was standing behind me in the queue. Suddenly, he leaned forward and asked how old I was.

'Fifteen,' I told him.

'You're having a hard time, I can see…'

He paused, then raised those wonderful blue eyes and asked, 'What will you do when you return to Lithuania?'

We both laughed and looked meaningfully at each other. I understood. Poor man, he wanted to comfort me by suggesting that we'd all survive and return to our former lives in Lithuania.

He was the first person to reach out to me with words of comfort.

Maybe we will survive, or some of us will, and return to our homes in Finland or Lithuania. Few of the workers are typical Finns – cultured, friendly, neat and longing to go home. Maybe ten in all. The rest are Finns in name only. They've been Russianized, they worship the Soviet order

A steamer with deportees on one of the
channels in the Lena River Delta.

and were happy with their former lives in Leningrad or on the outskirts of the city on collective farms. They have never seen Finland, nor do they speak the language. From the time of Peter I, such people have lived in and around Petersburg. I found them coarse and uncultured. They did not like us nor we them.

We are now working the so-called gates. The ascent up the steep riverbank has been paved with horizontal logs, creating a road. And two sticks of wood, attached to each other in the form of a cross, have been embedded in a wooden block. The whole apparatus has been placed on the summit. Our brigade consists of sixteen people – four to each arm of the cross. By walking in a circle, we turn the arms of the cross all day. At the bottom of the hill, eight to ten logs are attached to a cable. As we walk round and round in a circle, we wind the cable around the block of wood, thus winching the logs up the hill. It no longer falls to us to shoulder the ropes.

When we were still hauling logs by sledge, Štarienė would pull just enough to keep the rope slightly taut. She had ulcers on her shoulders. Yet she would insist that I be thrown out of the brigade because I was only a child and wouldn't be able to work as hard as the rest of them. I felt so worthless. It was a real torment for me. I observe Aldona Nausėdienė – and that dignity of hers that comes from still feeling human. I think she'd sooner die of starvation than take something from someone else or demean herself by asking. She'd rather breathe her last than degrade another person. As I sit next to her and look around, I realize that all pretence, all those empty civilities and urban refinements with which we arrived, have dropped from us like borrowed rags. In this mortal battle for life and in the face of death, we appear as we truly are. The once amiable postmaster pilfers flour from the starving fellow sufferer who is lying next to him.

Our 'Sweetie' – that picture of gentility, the likeable and pious Genutė – cheats her friend, feeble Stasė Prapuolenienė, of her fair share of food. Say Genutė is dividing their ration in two. She cuts the bread in half and, holding both pieces behind her back – which I can see clearly – she tells her friend to pick a hand. If Stasė picks the right hand, and the right happens to be the larger piece, 'Sweetie' quickly switches pieces. I say nothing. It's a daily ritual. I haven't dared say anything to Stasė, because she worships her Tartuffe.

Our wounds have healed. We have built up our arm muscles. For sixteen hours a day, we walk in a circle. As a result, however, my head spins, and during the three to four hours that we get to sleep, I dream of the turning gyre. By eleven o'clock at night, we are sullen, withdrawn, exhausted. We drop into our barracks and immediately fall into a laboured sleep. Every night, the same dream – we turn the wheel, round and round and round. When we get up four hours later to return to work, our leg and arm muscles are still tense. And our heads are still heavy from repeating the same dream, the same circular walk, over and over again. But those sixteen hours of steady walking have kept the scurvy at bay. They've protected our legs – though not our faces. Our skin is chapped and rough, we're constantly spitting teeth, which wobble and break, our gums bleed and our saliva tastes of blood. The days are light and stealing is no longer possible.

We have been given a day off – the first after two months of log work. We're going on our own in search of firewood for ourselves. Each family sends one of its members to do the foraging. I have a slight fever of 37.5 degrees.

'Who's going from the Grinkevičius family?'

My brother, Juozas, does not volunteer. He wants to rest today. I'm feeling angry and hurt. Mum urges Juozas to join the group, but he just rolls his eyes peevishly and says, 'Let the females go. They have it easier than we do, yet still get the same rations.'

I pick up the rope and go out. It's April. The sun shines all day. Today is the first time I don't want to cover my face up to my eyes. The wind lashes at my cheeks and batters my ear flaps, which I deliberately left unfastened. Milė calls me crazy. Not that I need to be told, since I can no longer feel my cheeks, which have probably turned white with frostbite. I rub them with my glove as hard as I can until they begin to burn. Towards evening we start back from Ere Haios – facing a twelve-kilometre slog to pull our heavy logs. At one point, we are overtaken by a horse, which turns its head to look at its cohorts as it passes.

*

Easter Sunday. Even though all our Sundays are workdays, no one leaves for work today. The night before, Borisas, who now works for Sventicki, measuring logs and checking off deliveries with his one good hand, warned us to show up, or else...

You've turned into a slave-driver, Borisas.

Yet not a single Russian, Finn, Lithuanian, Kazakh or Cossack left for work. Nor did we arrange it that way, it just happened. At that moment, we stood as one. Afterwards, Sventicki boasted of having given us the day off.

We're off to find some firewood. The ice at the mouth of the mighty Lena sparkles. The glacier on the opposite shore sparkles. And with its dazzling snow, the tundra sparkles. The hill of Stolby is visible between the icebergs and gives the illusion of blocking our path ahead.

We stop to admire the splendour of the mighty and ruthless Arctic.

'Isn't it beautiful, Dalia?' asks Krikštanienė.

'Yes, beautiful,' I reply happily.

I am pleased to be addressed like an adult, treated as though I were an equal. And it's true that after the long polar night people have begun to regard me differently. I started out as an adolescent to whom no one paid any attention. Now they treat me like someone to be reckoned with and, it seems to me anyway, they even respect me. Maybe because I have always done my share of work, same as them.

Even Nausėdienė's attitude towards me seems to have changed, though the look she gives me is very sarcastic, and I shrink from it each time.

We work nights. The hours are shorter. Days are sixteen hours; nights, only twelve. But nights are harder because it's a struggle to stay awake. There's a bathhouse next door. One of its rooms has been turned into a barber's shop, the domain of Pusvaškienė and her young daughter, Gražutė. The diminutive, dark-haired, thirty-year-old hairdresser both lives and works there. Each night Gražutė sits on the logs and watches us walking the circle, heavily, painfully, without pausing. We wonder about her presence in the middle of the night. But yesterday, at four o'clock in the morning, we saw the tall, handsome factory manager's assistant come walking up. Pusvaškienė ran out coatless to meet him. He didn't say a word but picked her up in his arms like a child and, without quickening his step, carried her into the shop. Everyone condemns her for it, but she just gives them a wide grin and continues to carry on with the supervisors.

Today is 1 May: a working day. According to Sventicki, the entire Soviet Union will be working twice as hard. He urges us to produce twice our norm too. We even get a pleasant surprise to mark the occasion: an extra 200 grams of white bread. So at seven o'clock in the morning, everyone still alive in Trofimovsk goes out to work with the logs.

Even Sventicki and Duktov set off, doubtless to inspire us and raise morale. But a half-hour later and there isn't a gentleman in sight. Their aristocratic dispositions are obviously unsuited for rolling logs up a hill, and in driving snow no less. Around ten o'clock, a blizzard comes howling across the tundra. We can't see the logs. We can't see each other. The wind whips us off our feet. Work is impossible.

'When the weather's like this, it must be God himself telling us to celebrate the holiday,' says Irena Jankauskytė, a quick-witted and pretty girl.

But we're afraid to return to our barracks without permission. How disciplined we've become! We pile into the log pit, one on top of the other. At least it's shelter from the wind. Lying there, I remember another 1 May celebration, my only one before today. It was 1941, last year in Kaunas. The weather had already turned fairly warm. We were standing next to a group of actors and must have been staring because I could see Kipras Petrauskas saying something to the soprano Kardelienė, and laughing. Then he turned to us and bowed.

The snow has begun to pile up. I hear Krikštanienė's voice. I suppose we can leave. We start for home. The blizzard lashes our faces, pitches us forward, pulls us back, tosses us from side to side. We walk in a tight group, so as not to get lost separately and mistakenly head for the tundra. In this kind of weather, Allah himself couldn't find his way back. Tonight, at least, we'll be able to sleep to our heart's content.

The blizzard will probably be short; it seems to be coming in spurts. For a while, it howls madly, creates absolute turmoil, visibility nil, then all of a sudden it moans briefly and takes a break – as though exhausted from the nine long months of winter. During these short breaks, the outline of our barracks becomes visible – only metres away – and so, step by step, we manage to reach our 'palace'. But we're allowed just four hours of sleep before we are sent out again. Silently, we bind our feet in foot-wraps and, though we have some choice words we'd like to say out loud, we resist cursing. I have come to know the meaning of 'must'.

Today it is our turn at the steam baths. We are dismissed from work early – after only twelve hours. I am the first to finish bathing and leave. Back at the barracks, I prepare a surprise for everyone – I shovel out the entire window. I had to dig a hole two metres deep just to reach it. But when I go back inside, I am shocked. Disgusted. In the light of day, the barracks looks worse, more horrific even than I imagined. I begin to wish the snow would return to conceal everything again. The rags, the bodies huddled against each other, the floor... We don't need daylight! Our faces are jaundiced, our eyes sunken, our skeletons barely sheathed in skin. For a month now, Krikštanis has been suffering from dysentery. He is constantly on the pail.

We jerry-rig a shelf above our pallets and drape it with rags. Krikštanis has taken to sitting under his shelf – or rather his canopy.

'The Sultan 'neath his baldachin,' teases Milė Noreikienė, watching him.

Krikštanis no longer has the energy to walk.

I am lying on my pallet when a dog runs into the room. He must have broken free of a Yakut sledge. He howls as he thrashes about.

'Grab the dog. Tie him up,' shouts Krikštanis, his eyes blazing with fever and rolling in their sockets.

'The man's possessed.'

The women shudder in horror, while Krikštanis yells, 'Tie him up! Tie him up! I'll help. Throttle him! We can fry him, the fat… the meat…'

Krikštanis's eyes are huge, bulging. Using the last of his strength, he tries to slide off his pallet. Instead, he falls to the ground, gets up, sways, falls again… The terrified dog whines and tears around the room. We lift Krikštanis back onto his bunk. Suddenly, he calms down and mutters something. Once again, he takes his place under his canopy, as befitting the 'emperor' of the thirteenth barracks. He begins to gurgle and twitch. I walk over and sit down beside him. His wife hasn't returned from the baths yet. He mumbles incoherently.

One by one, people come back from the baths. We light the stove. We boil up our daily bread soup.

Two hours pass. Krikštanis lingers between life and death. Sometimes he thrashes about and gurgles. His eyes roll back into his head. Just last night I heard him comfort his wife: 'Well, we've made it to spring, Broniuk. The fishing season will begin. The two of us will fish from the boat. We'll eat till we're full, definitely, till we're full.'

He repeats the words 'till we're full', but it's obvious that they have lost their meaning for him.

'Stuttering like a billy goat – baa baa baa.' Grockis mocks the dying man while stirring his own soup. 'The soup will be nice and thick, Vytuk. Hey, give us a handful of peas, will you? The soup will be perfect.'

'He's an atheist, you see. That's why his soul is having such a hard time shaking off that body. The reason for all his grunting,' ventures wisecracking Milė Noreikienė, still hoping that Krikštanis will turn to God at the moment of death.

'You'd think he'd already be sensing the afterlife. It's his last chance to believe.'

'He's a communist. How the hell can he believe?'

Krikštanis has long since given up on the Soviet system and has cursed it a thousand times. Still his self-imposed exile from Lithuania will continue to baffle us. When we aren't boiling with indignation, we're laughing at the absurdity of it.

Krikštanienė weeps and wails, 'Daddy, why are you abandoning us? Oh, don't leave us here by ourselves.'

When she realizes that the end is near, she calls for her son, Ali, so that he'll remember the moment. But Ali shrieks, 'I'm scared of him! I'm scared of him!' and hides under the bunks at the other end of the room.

Krikštanis never does call on God, though many have waited expectantly for his conversion. At one point, he becomes lucid enough to call his wife, 'Broniuk!' Then he hangs on to her as if she were his lifeline. His is a difficult death. He cannot let go and his gurgling, his thrashing about and his death rattles join the clatter of pots and pans and the talk of pancakes. We have our own affairs to attend to. Some to die, others to squat on the pail, the rest to eat and chat.

All of a sudden, Krikštanis goes into a brief convulsion and dies. Blood and excrement stream out of his body. The stench is nauseating. The floor is wet with all kinds of bodily fluids, and the light of day falls on his naked corpse.

Conversation stops. We observe a moment of silence. One more victim.

'Where do I put him for the night?' asks Krikštanienė. She can't, after all, sleep with his corpse when it's so cramped.

'Stick him under the bunks.' Jasinskienė's voice has an edge to it, reminding everyone of the way Krikštanis mistreated Barniškienė's dead child.

Krikštanis's corpse spent the night on the floor.

'The emperor has been dethroned,' quips Milė, before slipping under her rags.

We have been brutalized, it occurs to me, totally brutalized.

'The two of us, Broniuk, we'll survive, we're young…' I can still hear Krikštanis whispering to his wife.

The thirteenth barracks is asleep.

A handsome and pleasant youth in his school uniform comes to see us each day that we work at our 'galley' wheel. One of his feet is heavily bound. He settles on the logs and sits there for hours looking out over the wide channels of the Lena River, the hills on the horizon, the rock of Stolby, which seems to lie directly in our path when we head back to the barracks, and the vast, barren tundra. Each time we swing past him on our creaking wheel, we stare longingly at his clean face and his apparently brand-new blue secondary-school uniform. How has he managed to hang on to it? Most bartered theirs for food ages ago. He gets 800 grams of bread without having to work. We almost envy him.

Turns out that he had been fishing with Grockis one day, checking the nets under the ice, when he accidentally stuck his foot into the ice hole. Had he run home immediately, the foot might not have frozen, might just have suffered some frostbite. But Grockis, after first swearing at him, said in his usual unruffled voice, 'Hm, your foot isn't going anywhere, while the ice holes will certainly freeze over. Hm, we can't stop now, we have to finish checking all of them.'

And so they did.

Mindaugas returned to his barracks later that day dragging his foot. Half of it had frozen and developed gangrene. The Yakuts agreed to take him to Tiksi for an amputation, but they threw him off the dog sledge just outside Trofimovsk. He spent the winter bedridden in the barracks. The gangrene did not progress and the dead flesh eventually dropped off, though the foot did become deformed when some of the bones repositioned themselves under his foot. But spring found him alive and, despite coming down with scurvy and having his legs seize up, he recovered. Many years later, Mindaugas and I would take a turn on the dance floor more than once – though

Deportees repairing fishing nets in Trofimovsk, 1949.

he did drag his foot during the foxtrot. A small bone had remained permanently fixed under the sole of his foot.

Today, 14 May, another party of deportees has left for the Laptev coast in Bobrovsk, which is 150 kilometres away. A woman from our barracks, Vincė Sidaravičiūtė, otherwise known as Mrs Daunorienė, as she prefers to be called, has joined the group. In Kaunas she lived with a policeman named Daunoras and worked in the hospital kitchen. When Daunoras was deported, loving him as she did, she went along with him, thinking they would stay together. She was a simple, warm-hearted twenty-five-year-old. Her love and devotion to him give her more right to call herself Mrs Daunorienė than if they had been joined at the altar. We never tire of her kitchen stories. We beg her over and over again to tell us what the patients were fed at the hospital. When she comes to the part about throwing the leftovers into the open cesspit, we gasp in unison and curse furiously. If only we had sewage pits like that around here, we'd certainly know how to sift through them for food. During the whole time of our deportation, Vincė lived with Žukienė, but when she got dysentery and soiled herself up to her ears, Žukienė threw her out of their shared pallet. Not that it helped much because the stench and the lice left behind continued to besiege Žukienė.

But Vincė did not die of dysentery, though a hundred people out of a hundred had no doubt that she would. Thanks to Dr Samodurov, who pumped her full of vitamins, she rose from the dead. When she agreed to join the fishing expedition to Bobrovsk, we all thought that she'd taken leave of her senses. This shadow of a human being, who could barely walk, intended to hike 150 kilometres. A journey that would involve trudging through snowdrifts, manoeuvring across sharp palings in the snow without a clear road to follow except for the occasional pawprint from a passing dog. If she ever fell behind, no one was going to risk their life to save her. What would happen then? But Vincė had made up her mind. She was going regardless.

'At least I'll eat my fill of fish. And if I die along the way like a dog, no great loss, I'd be dead here too.'

Her logic was iron-clad, so we said nothing.

'But if she does make it, and eats all that fish, and her stomach is full every day...' Grockis contemplates the prospect out loud. 'She'll fry herself an oily sturgeon...'

Our mouths water at the vision. Well, it'll be interesting to see how this all turns out.

About twenty people, including Samodurov and five Cossacks, take off for Bobrovsk. Two dog sledges carrying equipment and other things head up the slow-moving, exhausted caravan of people. Vincė's red hood soon disappears from view. I cannot believe her strength. The Arctic validates only the strong, not the living dead. That night I dream of Vincė in a field of flowers.

On 15 May we get our last blizzard of the season. No one doubts that Vincė will perish.

In Trofimovsk the snow is already melting. It's mid-May and the beginning of an early spring. Some of the Russians who have been knocking about the Arctic since 1930 say they've never seen such an early spring. Trofimovsk is turning into one large cesspit, which hardly bears imagining. The barracks are surrounded by enormous piles of excrement and other human waste, including general trash and rags. Nearly a year's worth. Each day, more and more of it emerges from under the snow cover. One gets the impression that we have been living on piles of manure, because we can hardly move without stepping into it. How come we didn't all die of typhus? Now this human waste is flowing into the lake from which we draw our water, which has turned brown with shit.

'I have reached the conclusion that medical science has it wrong when it claims that microbes are harmful organisms. If they were, we'd have crapped our guts out long ago,' muses Grockis.

Supervisor Mavrin makes his way through the barracks, shaming its inhabitants.

'I've seen all kinds of people, but pigs like you – never. Even the Chinese are a cleaner lot.'

He wants us to carry the waste on stretchers to the shore. We consent, but ask to be paid. Mavrin refuses. Bastard, too cheap to spend a few government kopeks. Armed with stretchers and pickaxes, after work hours we make for the piles of manure. 'Picking at shit,' Milė calls it. We work slowly, grudgingly, malingering as best as we can. Seeing that the piles are not shrinking, the next day Mavrin sends in five brigades, which work for pay.

Grockis drags home some sort of blanket. He found it in a pile of excrement, most likely saved it from a corpse.

'I'll wash it out, it'll be fine.' And he was right – the blanket did turn out fine. Probably it had belonged to a Finn. But during the time it took Grockis to wash it, you could have gagged on the stench.

Today is my birthday. We have finished hauling logs and the management gives us our first day off. We sit around our stove, soaked to the skin. Since yesterday night, it has been raining hard. Like the snow in winter that would come into the room through the gaps in the ceiling, now the rain is coming down on us in torrents. Our rags – our so-called bedlinen – are literally afloat on our bunks. And on the floor the water is up to our ankles. I always took pride in the fact that my birthday – 28 May – occurred during the most beautiful time of year. The orchards were in bloom, the air was fragrant. Each birthday was a happy occasion, and in the evening, after my girlfriends had left, I would stand at the open window for a long time, unable to get enough of the beauty outside. That's when I fell in love with life, with all that was beautiful in it – a love that has survived till now.

I remember my thirteenth birthday perfectly. There were just the four girlfriends. Mum had prepared the table with all kinds of tortes and sweets. But the girls were shy and wouldn't eat. Mum would urge them to try one thing or another, but they would only answer, 'No, thanks, I'm fine. Thank you.'

Yet no sooner did Mum leave the room than the tortes vanished in seconds, and all that remained were the sweet wrappers in the vases. When she returned, there was very little left on the table – instead there was icing on our chins and chocolate on our lips. It had not taken much urging. When my friends finally left, Dad walked quietly into the room. He gave me a kiss and, putting his arm around me, joined me at the open window. I can still remember what he said.

'Life, Dalia, isn't all fun and games. Life is a battle. Prepare for it. You don't want to be a scaredy cat.' After a short pause, he added, 'What I'm trying to say, dear girl, is never betray your conscience.'

I looked up at him: his face was lit by the last rays of the sun, his eyes were moist and his lips trembled. He wanted to say more. But the world smelt of blossoms. I remember thinking, no, life is beautiful, not hard, and it will always be like a splendid dream. I couldn't imagine life being anything but magical.

The rain is pouring down my face, my hair, my back, my stomach. Water, water everywhere! The last of the snow is melting on the tundra. Our red-brick barracks has risen from its snowy grave. The sounds of rain and wind occasionally blend with the honking of wild geese overhead. The Yakuts are hunting on the tundra. Yesterday, on his way home from the hunt, one of them reported seeing a woman's corpse. Given his description of her, we guessed it might be Baltrukonienė. Today, eight Lithuanians went out with stretchers to bring her home. Regina Stalauskaitė urged me to join them, but I refused as I was afraid. Not because she was dead, but because she'd be frozen. It's the frozen ones that horrify me. Towards evening, a slow procession appeared in the distance. A stretcher on the shoulders, a woman on the stretcher. The bearers were deathly pale and could hardly lift their feet as they walked. They complained that she was inhumanly heavy. They had found her face down five kilometres away, her stockings bunched around her ankles. When they turned her over, she started bleeding from the nose, as if she had just died. Her cheeks were pink, no sign of decay. She had been lying under the snow, frozen solid for exactly five months. Had the Yakut not found her, she would have lain there till she rotted, just like Albertas, Dzikas and a hundred other prisoners and fishermen who came to early graves on the vast, uncharted tundra this winter. Her gold watch and the small gold cross around her neck were not found. This led some to believe that she'd been robbed, especially as her stockings were torn and bunched around her ankles, and her fur jacket unbuttoned. Nonsense! She must have realized immediately that she'd passed the bakery, that the blizzard had disorientated her and was carrying her further and further into the land of ice and tundra. What must she have thought? What screams of anguish erupted from her breast when she realized that she was heading for an icy grave and leaving behind her shivering four-year-old, Jaunutis? What must the mother's heart have felt when her hands and feet grew numb and her heart began to give out? They say that when people get lost in a blizzard, they go insane: they begin to burn up, hallucinate, discard their mittens, shawl, hat. Baltrukonienė must have been tearing off her clothes for the same reason.

Her son, Jaunutis, was brought to the morgue to see his mother. Dr Griko helped herself to the dead woman's fur jacket, which Baltrukonienė had worn for five months in her icy grave. How is Misiūnienė any worse? She stole the sheets from cadavers because she was starving. What is Griko's excuse? She already has fifteen suitcases filled with Lithuanian goods.

Flooding is now the most pressing danger facing us, because Trofimovsk is on a small island at the mouth of the Lena. It is completely surrounded by channels and rivulets. Our ashen-faced supervisors are racing back and forth along the riverfront, while the Lena is bursting its banks. We are ordered to stay awake all night. What for? There aren't any boats to evacuate us. Not that boats would be any use. Trofimovsk is a tiny island on a delta. When the giant icebergs jam the river in their passage to the Laptev Sea, nothing will be left of our island, it will be ground into shreds. I am awakened in the night by a furious din – a booming, crashing noise. The icebergs are on the move. The gong is ringing non-stop, which means that the water is rising. Our island is being flooded. But none of us budge. We have become indifferent even to death. If I am destined to die, I will die. It is out of my hands. Our supervisors don't seem that keen on dying; they're in a panic.

I raise my head and burst out laughing. Milė is sitting up on her pallet and leaning against the wall. She's got two crimson ribbons in her hair, which she's just combed. And lipstick. She's wearing lipstick.

'Noreikienė, are you crazy?'

'I want to look nice, at least, before I die. If I have to drown, it'll be in ribbons.'

Oh, that Milė, that ragbag of flirtation, our elegant secretary's wife at the Warsaw consulate, she has not lost her spunk yet. Even in the face of death, she can't stop joking.

The icebergs are at our door. One more second and our edifice of brick, moss and soil will be crushed like a matchbox. But death is not in the hand we are dealt. The water begins to recede. It leaves behind chunks of colliding ice along the shore that reach halfway up the side of our barracks. Violet crystals. We chip at the ice with pickaxes and enjoy fresh water.

For seven days and seven nights, we listen to the passage of the ice. Lumbering, colliding, the icebergs pulverize each other when they meet. Our ears have gone deaf from the sound. We see ice floes floating by, strewn with stuff, including a blanket and several corpses. Maybe it's Albertas and his friends? Hasn't the North claimed enough victims for one winter?

Twice more we see bodies drift out to sea on ice floes. One of them also carries a barking dog. What a multitude of bodies the Lena must have carried into the Arctic Ocean, considering that the channel flowing past our island is only one of thousands that empties into the Laptev Sea!

I've now fainted twice and had a nosebleed while rolling logs. I frequently feel light-headed. Dr Samodurov examined me. He said I have tuberculosis. He ordered me to stop working altogether. Each day I feel worse. Don't tell me I'm going to die after all? The doctor told me to apply to the commission for permission to move to Yakutsk.

There is now a great deal of activity in Trofimovsk. Since the waters have become navigable, the first convoy of barges will be arriving soon. The fishing season is upon us. Nor is there any talk of letting us leave the polar region. Everyone who has survived the winter and can still walk is being sent fishing. Those who are absolutely unsuited to fishing – the invalids – are put to work processing fish. There are hundreds of tonnes of frozen fish in Bobrovsk and Tumat waiting to be processed. Now that it's spring, some Lithuanians and Finns have organized themselves into fishing cooperatives or guilds. Stankevičius and Steponavičienė have been going from barracks to barracks talking up their co-op, which would pay its fishermen in goods or money for whatever fish they catch. As long as there is fish to be caught, they'd live royally off what they earned. But if there is no fish – starvation. Anyone who signed on got twenty kilos of flour in advance. That was such an incentive to people who were still on the verge of starvation that many joined just to get something to eat. Almost no one joined from our barracks, except the Totoraitis family and Barniškienė. The joiners ridiculed us for hanging back, telling us we'd be sorry. I wavered briefly, but my brother made an obscene joke at the co-op's expense and categorically refused to join, so I didn't either. The cooperatives organized the fishermen into brigades and the brigades into sectors. The first cutters ferried the various sectors to specific fishing locations. I completed a course in accounting and was posted to a job in Bobrovsk. Juozas was appointed to a state-run fishing crew – the Cossack brigade. They earn a flat fee of 220 rubles a month, but very little for the fish. However, they're entitled to ration cards, so even if they come back empty they won't starve. However, if the fish are plentiful they won't earn any more for the ones they catch. Their brigade leader is Saulevičienė's husband, Tuminas.

A fishing brigade consists of five fishermen using a relatively small 300-metre net. The fishermen toss the net out eight to twelve times a day and work sixteen- to twenty-hour days, after which they bring the fish back to Trofimovsk, a twenty-kilometre journey. Tuminas is always in a hurry to get back to his wife and impatient with his crew on the return trip. He claims his wife pines for him when he's away. Juozas says he looks like an orang-utan and makes fun of him. Tuminas maintains that during the Civil War he chopped off more than one head like a cabbage.

I'd already met the Estonian Kespaiko, the stockroom supervisor. Back in Estonia, as a member of the outlawed Communist Party, he fled to Tartu. Needless to say, he quickly recovered from his political leanings, but by then it was too late. There was no way to return to his homeland. Since 1922, he and his wife, Vera Pavlovna, have been bouncing from one Soviet city and one Soviet gold mine to another. This winter in March I worked in his cooperative, making folders out of cardboard boxes the Americans had used for packing tinned goods. Kespaiko gave me flour to make glue. He would also take me to the stockroom, measure out three kilos of flour and whisper in my ear, 'Take this home.' The flour I used for making glue was distributed separately. The folders I made weren't very good; they were shoddy and lopsided. I worked slowly, but Kespaiko didn't fire me. He let me pass the time in a warm office and eat pancakes. He once told me, 'I'd give you a whole sack of flour, but it wouldn't save you from starvation and I'd end up in the nick, because your people like to gossip.'

I ran into Kespaiko recently. He told me that he had handed his job as stockroom supervisor over to someone else and was moving to Bobrovsk to take charge of a fishing sector. He wanted his crew to be Lithuanians, so he was hand-picking them. That's how I got to Bobrovsk. One beautiful afternoon, when the Lena was remarkably quiet and smooth as a mirror, the cutter *Komsomolets* left Trofimovsk towing a barge packed with supplies, nets, salt, lots of people and fishing boats.

Slowly, for the last time, we sailed past the brick barracks, the wooden barracks, the earthen dwellings and the hill that had consumed hundreds of corpses. Liuda, who had buried her brother and her mother, began to weep. I noticed that almost everyone was weeping, their eyes fixed silently on that monstrous graveyard, that 'monument not built by human hands'. Personally, I feel that a great weight has been lifted from me. I am still alive, and my mother is sitting next to me.

Famine has become a thing of the past. We are sailing to eat fish. We are sailing for a better future.

For the second day in a row, the cutter rumbles monoto-nously on, the barge rocks behind, and islands and islets that have never seen a human footprint appear. I marvel how the local Yakut at the helm can find his way. As we draw closer to the sea, the channels branch off into other channels, which number in the hundreds, even thousands. Driftwood litters the islands' shores. Year after year, the river has been carrying driftwood downstream from for-ested places. Occasionally, a herd of deer swim by, their antlers visible like steeples above the water. Here and there on the bleak and barren tundra, we see icebergs that haven't melted yet, even though it's already July. One can navigate these waters for a month without meeting another living soul. Suddenly, we hear the motor stop. The barge and the fishing skiffs continue to drift with the current. The barge begins to spin slowly in a circle. We are in a channel so wide that its shores are out of sight. The anchor eventually puts an end to our twirling. The cutter cannot be repaired. At the risk of getting lost, the Lithuanian fishermen unhook their boat and begin to row in the direction of Bobrovsk. Their navigator is a Yakut who can tell which way the sea lies by sniffing the air. Another skiff navigates in the oppo-site direction against the current towards Trofimovsk. The authorities need to be notified of our setback. Time slows even more. We have entered the season of polar days – of the 'white nights' when the sun never sets. We can't tell how many days pass. Some say it is Sunday and others, Thursday.

A storm has been pounding us for a while. The barge rocks and spins, while the waves roll across her open, unprotected deck, dunking us all in the black, salty water of the Laptev Sea. It has become unspeakably cold. We shiver like dogs. At any moment, the wind might rip the clothes from our backs or sweep us right off the barge. It rains intermittently. We have no shelter, no cover at all. We are completely exposed to the sky and the sea feels dangerously close.

We have finished the bread and are tormented by hunger. When will the other cutter, the *Tikhy*, arrive? Even the *Tikhy* is a sputtering wreck that is forever breaking down. That Yakut wasn't kidding when he told supervisor Mavrin, '*Tvoy kater tolko pokoynikov srat vozit.*' – 'The only thing your cutter is good for is hauling the dead out to shit.' A fish-processing plant, spread some 200 to 300 kilometres along the seashore, owns only two dilapidated cutters. Perhaps the fishing skiff got lost on the way and the news about us never reached Trofimovsk? Kespaiko takes it upon himself to distribute a kilo of flour per person as well as a tin of food, which we eat immediately. The flour is more problematic: we eat it raw, because we have nowhere to bake it. We're afraid the storm will never end, the cutter will never arrive and we will die here, frozen solid on an open barge in the black waters of an Arctic sea. Frania is also on board, sailing to Bobrovsk to see a patient. Teeth clenched, she suffers silently. A Yakut girl lies next to us. She came aboard as she was, wearing only her padded jacket. By now she has turned blackish green from the cold. I throw my red winter coat over her. She mumbles something, probably 'thanks', and places a large chunk of sugar in my mother's hand. By whose will have we been gathered in this place? What circumstances have brought such varied people together, united us in a shared destiny and thrust us into the middle of the sea? A party of us board a rowing boat to search for land. Three to five kilometres later, we disembark on an island. A few hundred metres inland, we notice a wooden monument and two crosses. The inscription is still legible: 1905 or 1895, Barantol. So this is where the Swedish explorer of the North, Barantol, came to an early end. One of the caskets had been chopped up – apparently, by someone who also found himself, for whatever reason, in this desolate place. The remains of a campfire are still visible and a skeleton lies in the distance.

There is no driftwood to be seen. We find over a dozen wild goose eggs and row back. It is hard to imagine that in Lithuania people have shed their coats and the sun is shining, that somewhere it is summer, that it is warm, that the crashing waves of the Arctic Ocean cannot be heard or freeze the blood, that somewhere there is life.

We can't tell how long we've been waiting. Feels like months. Finally, we see smoke on the horizon. It's the *Tikhy*. It's drawing closer. We can see the unmistakable figure of Ernestas Vanagas waving.

A month has passed since we arrived in Bobrovsk. The settlement has one small log house – that's the store. Misha Butakov, the storekeeper, lives there. And now Kespaiko lives with him. An office has been set up in a tiny yurt. Several hundred metres away are two more yurts for the workers.

The Finns are in one, the Lithuanians in the other. That is the whole of Bobrovsk. We work in twelve-hour shifts. Even though our yurt is small, we all fit: Regina, Liuda (who is getting prettier by the day, and she knows it, you can see it in her eyes, she's aware of her charm), Dovydaitienė with her small daughter, Balčiuvienė and her two girls, the cooper Rimas Rimkevičius and Steponavičienė. The yurt is square. The walls are constructed of vertical logs split in half lengthwise and staked into the ground. They're covered with moss. Sand sifts through the cracks in the ceiling and falls on our heads – which is not too unpleasant. The ceiling will hold back a shower; it is only the downpours that come through. But we have a table. This gives us immense pleasure. We have not had one before anywhere. Finally, a place to put our dishes when we're making pancakes or frying fish. And a table at which to eat. The yurt also has two small windows. We're very contented. Most important of all, we are no longer hungry! There are around 300 tonnes of frozen fish in the cellar, all caught this winter. But what idiots to site a cellar in a marsh, where it fills with water! This means hacking at the frozen fish with pickaxes and tossing it up in chunks to defrost. Gutting fish is disgusting work: the stench. Some of the fish has turned yellow and is cold as ice, and some has decayed outright. Our fingers sink into the flesh, the bones have separated from the meat. But our supervisor instructs us to go ahead and salt it anyway, so we do. What business is it of ours…? No one seems to care whether it's edible or not. When the putrid fish is placed in the barrel with fresh fish, everything rots. You actually have to hold your nose just to walk past a station where the fish is being processed. But we get used to it. After we've left the fish lying in salt for a while, we wash them in brine, sort them and put them in barrels. We then pack them down firmly, as we're supposed to, and the coopers seal the barrels.

Most of them leak, even the brand-new ones just arrived from the workshops. Even these are like sieves. The negligence is terrible. The barrels are supposedly manufactured under the supervision of specialists and inspected by a commission. When they arrive in Trofimovsk, our supervisors are there to receive them, as are the managers in Bobrovsk. Yet every one of them is clearly junk.

'Vidish li,' says the waggish Yakut to me, Rimkevičius's right-hand man, 'kazhdy byot na kolichestvo, a kachestvo… kachestvo – veshch vtorostepennaya.' – 'You see, everyone tries to produce as much as he can, so quality… well, quality is of secondary importance.' Then he winks and laughs.

I find the Yakuts rather quick-witted. I can't understand why other people call them primitive.

When we first salt the fish, it already has an odour. After time spent in the leaky barrels, which do not hold the liquid, it decomposes completely. There are hundreds of tonnes in the cellar waiting to be processed, to say nothing of the fresh fish, which can't wait. Thus a whole year's catch is systematically allowed to putrefy. All the supervisors are on site, fully present, yet none of them seems particularly concerned. Except for Grunia, who takes her job seriously. She's the brining specialist; it was only during the winter months that she temporarily assisted in the store. She's a decent sort. When we take home the greasy fish guts and pike livers to fry them for their oil, Grunia turns a blind eye, even though she is required to collect a certain amount of oil herself. Mavrin once came in to check her casks of fish oil and found them half empty. He asked her what had happened. Grunia blushed and lost her composure – she can't lie to save her life – then stammered, 'For some reason, this fish isn't very oily…'

'It's a winter fish – of course it's oily. You're mistaken,' Mavrin spluttered through teeth clamped on a black cigarette holder.

There was, actually, a lot of fish oil available, enough to drink our fill if we wanted. I once drank half a litre – and my stomach survived. Every day we smuggled a fish out in our trousers or sleeves. The only one afraid to steal was Marytė Sirutytė. Her mother reproached her for it all the time. Balčiuvienė and I would carry home a sturgeon twice a day – one at lunchtime and one after work. She would pretend that 'nature was calling' and head for the beach. On the way, she would grab the fish and hide it under her blood-and-guts-splattered apron. Then, as she made her way down the riverbank, she would slip it into her trousers. My technique was to wait till the last minute of work and then stick the sturgeon or omul, tail first, up the sleeve of my padded jacket, resting its head in my hand. Then we'd march triumphantly back to our yurt. The Finns, the Lithuanians, the Russians – all the women smuggled out two or three fish daily. We often found ourselves marching past our supervisors, who eyed us suspiciously, but our clothes were so wretched and we looked so appalling – our padded outfits hung on us like sacks – that they failed to detect anything.

Frozen fish is easier to carry than fresh because of its frozen scales; fresh fish is slippery. When pulled out of the sleeve, it leaves the entire arm slimy. Balčiuvienė bemoans the fact that by the time she reaches the yurt, some part of her anatomy – it happens every time – has frostbite. We laugh ourselves silly over it! Sometimes we laugh so hard remembering all the details that we choke on our mouthfuls of fish. At first, we thought we'd never eat our fill. No matter how large the fish or how much fat it was floating in, we'd wolf it down immediately. Bobrovsk has no bakery, yet our ration consists of flour. So our pancakes, deep-fried in oil, turn into balls of fried dough. This is our honeymoon. We've all changed. My TB has disappeared. Whenever someone wanted to tease me before, they'd call me consumptive. But here my muscles became hard and each day I felt more of my strength return. Mum filled out and became more cheerful. Dovydaitienė, who walked with a stoop in Trofimovsk, began to straighten her back. The colour returned to her cheeks, as did the fire in her eyes. We had all turned into hermaphrodites and scarecrows. Now the women became women again and the men became men.

After work, Kespaiko would frequently pay us a visit. Himself an Estonian, he liked Lithuanians. At first, we were careful around him. Whenever we saw him coming, we would hide the frying pans with their sizzling fish under

Abandoned fishing yurt built 1943–6 by Lithuanian
deportees on an island on the Lena. Image taken in 1989.

our bunks. On one occasion, he crossed our threshold while we were still cooking. He asked how we were doing.

'Fine,' we said.

'Are you sure? You need a better diet. You're frail and weak. Look at your hands, they're chapped. You should rub them with oil.'

Dovydaitienė pulls out her frying pan from under the bunk and puts it on the stove. She'd been melting fat.

'I've got oil.'

'You also need fish,' says Kespaiko.

'We don't have any money.'

'The cellar is filled with fish. Help yourselves.'

Gradually, frying pans begin to appear on the stove, sizzling cheerfully. The room smells of mouth-watering sturgeon. Kespaiko smiles. He is the only one to see the human beings underneath the rags, the only one not to treat us like cattle or slaves. He understands everything and looks sadly at us, shaking his head: '*Vo chto vas prevratili?*' – 'What have they turned you into?'

He despises our idiot bosses. He witnessed the systematic annihilation that took place last winter and he tormented himself over his inability to stop that human meat-mincer.

He says to us, '*Etot Sventicki, bog Trofimovska, on izdevayetsya nad vami, on kholuy ot prirody, a takiye lyudi, kogda imeyut vlast – tirany. Potomu, chto im zavidno, chto zhyli vy kogda-to inache.*' – 'This Sventicki, the god of Trofimovsk, he sneers at you. He's a boot-licker by nature, and when people like that get hold of power they become tyrants. Because they resent the fact that you did not always live like this.'

At each visit, Kespaiko asks us to sing some Lithuanian songs. He especially likes 'How Beautiful Thou Art, Beloved Land of Our Fathers'. He bows his head to hide his tears and listens. He sits like that for a long time, while we sing the sad, beautiful songs of our distant homeland. Nor are his the only tears in the room.

'Your songs so remind me of Estonia,' he says, looking through our tiny window at the colossal emptiness of the tundra. 'It's been twenty years. When will I see her again?'

Then, stooping slightly, he exits without a word and, walking slowly, disappears into the distance. But not in the direction of home. He wades out into the depths of the tundra like a man forsaken.

Vincė is also in Bobrovsk salting fish. She did not perish, as we had expected her to, though she has had a rough journey.

She had made it only halfway to Bobrovsk when she became so exhausted that she could only crawl. She couldn't feel her feet for being so tired, and grew so weak that when she fell she could no longer get up. The snow coming down on her with blizzard force was wet. But not very cold, for it was already 16 May. The caravan left her behind, fifty kilometres shy of Bobrovsk. She lay on the ice for twelve hours during the blizzard. She said she dreamt of being back in the barracks, that we offered her tea. Strangely enough, people who are freezing begin to hallucinate – they imagine themselves drinking hot coffee. Meanwhile, her fellow travellers reached Bobrovsk. Samodurov had come to visit a patient and, although mortally exhausted himself, he ordered a sledge to be brought and left with the dogs to find Vincė himself. For several hours, he searched the place where they had left her, but without luck. He thought she might have stood up and lost her way on the tundra. At last he discovered her under the snow. The doctor poured some spirit into her mouth and felt her feet, certain that they'd have to be amputated. But she had absolutely no frostbite. He and the dogs brought her back to Bobrovsk. This happy ending astonished everyone. The story of Vincė's adventure made the rounds of the entire factory. 'That is one superior woman,' the Russians marvelled. In Bobrovsk, Vincė ate her fill, regained her curves and got married, or rather shacked up, as they said here, with a Cossack. He is old, homely, lazy and – one must say – mentally undistinguished, but Vincė likes him. Everyone has an opinion on the subject. Žukienė claims that Vincė sold herself for a crust of bread; others, that one cannot expect anything better from a whore (having in mind her living with Daunoras without the benefit of matrimony); still others were genuinely perplexed. They watched her continue to work alongside the rest of us – hands and clothes eaten away by salt – and would ask with puzzled candour, 'But Vincė, why did you marry the guy, if you still have to work night and day?' The rest of us, out of respect for the woman and her choices, said nothing.

The one who used to infuriate me the most was Digrevičienė. Her fishing partner was a Yakut. The two lived together in a small yurt twenty kilometres from Bobrovsk and I bet they did not spend their nights saying the rosary. Yet she had the gall to lecture Vincė. When Zigmas Steponavičius made snide remarks to Digrevičienė, she would merely strike her favourite pose – hands in pockets and hat cocked rakishly on her head – then shrug her shoulders and, smiling brazenly, say to him, 'You don't know, Zigmas, so go ahead and prove that I'm living with him!'

What can you say to an argument like that? But we all knew what was going on. Her partner learned to speak Lithuanian, while Digrevičienė learned Yakut. As for Vincė? Vincė kept quiet, she had no way to retaliate verbally. Her problem was that, unlike some of the others, she did not hide her relationship with the Cossack. She broke her silence only once, after the taunting finally got to her. She flung the fish she'd been washing into the briny vat and with a quavering voice said, 'What do you want from me? You're the whores! Because you do it in secret. I do it openly because I love him. I love him, he's a good man. Besides, it's my decision and mine to give to whomever I like. I don't need to ask you for permission.'

That pretty much shut everyone up. She's young, she's human, she has a right to love anyone she pleases. She's not like Saulevičienė and the others, who have been trading their bodies for flour, literally, because they feared starvation, they feared hardship. I remember what Vincė replied when we suggested that she will probably get married too: 'I do not plan to sell myself for a kilo of flour.' She suffered greatly through the famine, endured a bloody bout of dysentery, crawled to Bobrovsk on her hands and knees, and when she recovered and regained her womanliness, why should anyone be surprised that she fell in love? If she loves him, he is handsome to her and lovable. We meddle too much in other people's affairs, without any right to do so.

In Bobrovsk during the summer months the fish keep to the deeper waters. Fishing with a large net is a waste of energy. The twenty-five-metre nets are more appropriate, though they have to be checked daily for what turns out to be nothing but sturgeon, and there isn't a lot of that either. A cutter arrives from Trofimovsk with our supervisors on board. The foreman of the Lithuanian cooperative, Stankevičius, is among them. They inform us that the fish are abundant in Tumat. Each net there catches between two and two and a half tonnes. The Lithuanian fishing co-ops have already earned a tonne of flour and a hundred or so kilos of sugar. So while the fish are still plentiful, the cutter has arrived to transport nearly all the fishermen to Tumat. Five boats with two fishermen each will stay behind in Bobrovsk; they can bring in around sixty kilos of fish a day. Since we are no longer hungry, we are now eager for fresh catch. That is all we steal now. Some of us take the fish while it is still on the stretchers and hide it between the barrels. Others nick it from the tables after it's been gutted or after it has already been washed or after it has arrived for salting. As for the rest, they pull it right out of the barrel and drag it home – a salted fish ready to eat. Steponavičienė goes one better. At night she sets out with an empty sack and returns with it half filled. Her fisherman son, Zigmas, turns in the fish he's caught for hard currency and food vouchers, while at night his mother steals it back, rinses out the salt and smokes it in her small, personal smoker. Steponavičienė swipes anything that is out of place: old pans, torn sacks, rope, nails – in short, everything. One day, we notice that she is making herself some footwear out of rope. So we start filching it too. Since the stockroom has no lock on it, we help ourselves to the rope and knit it into shoes. The authorities begin to notice that the stockroom is out of rope and that the Lithuanians are wading through mud in rope shoes, like medieval serfs. They're furious, but since they haven't caught anyone in the act, they say nothing. On one occasion, Yustov and the Černeckis girl brought in some gorgeous sturgeon. Our eyes lit up. Then, after work, we all carried home a sturgeon. I hid mine under my jacket, and I used my hand, which I placed in my pocket, to prop it up by the gills. But on my way back, I ran into Smelkov. I felt a rush of heat and my heart began to pound.

'Good day, Dalia.'

'Good day, Konstantin Pavlovich.'

All of a sudden, I felt the ground sliding out from under me: the big, meaty tail of the sturgeon had just poked through the top of my unbuttoned jacket and was flapping its tail like a fan at my neck. By a miracle, Smelkov did not notice. He was distracted by the bookkeeper, who had just summoned him. With bullet speed, I took off in the direction of the yurts. I paused behind the first one I reached, pulled out my prize and tossed it behind a pile of twigs. The fat, hefty sturgeon was nearly a metre long; half of him had been dragging on the ground. He was still alive, even though his innards had already been removed. The sturgeon continues to twitch and its heart continues to beat by itself for about five minutes outside the body. I caught up with Dovydaitienė and both of us fell to the ground in hysterics. What a spectacle. She had put a live sturgeon down her trousers and it was moving around, making her wriggle like a serpent and grab at her crotch, first at the front, then at the back. Eventually, we reached home – in the case of Dovydaitienė, with her trouserful intact. What a feast we had that day. The sturgeon sizzled in its own fat. Mine weighed about eight kilos and between the two of us we poured off two and a half litres of oil. We fried dough, we drank coffee with condensed milk, we ate chocolate. All of it supplied by Butakov on orders from above.

According to Sirutienė, life is different on a full stomach. When the yurt is cold, when a storm is blowing, when we're drenched by the rain and our wet firewood won't burn, she is convinced that we will never return, that death is our only future. But once the fire begins to roar and the stove turns red hot, the sturgeon crackles in the pan, the stomach feels full, she becomes more optimistic about the future: maybe we'll return after all, perhaps we will survive. It's often like that.

So our polar days with the 'midnight sun' drag on. We lose track of time by days, even weeks.

Suddenly, like a shot out of nowhere, our quiet life came to an end. Kespaiko had made a short trip to Trofimovsk. Then one night he returned to Bobrovsk with Vera Chorinova. The next morning, he summoned Rimkevičius and instructed him to construct two barrels that didn't leak a single drop. For some time now, he said, he'd been planning an expedition, hoping to find some good fishing spots thirty kilometres away. En route he wanted to get some hunting in as well. All day you could hear Kespaiko in the store hammering lead into gunshot. My intuition told me that he was preparing for a grand exit. After lunch break, Liuda did not return to work. She was collecting her things, getting ready to leave us. Dovydaitienė, Balčiuvienė and I were resting after our night shift. We asked her where she was going.

'I am going to marry Erhard Modestovich Kespaiko.'

'But Liuda, he's got a wife.'

'So what? She's there, I'm here.'

When she finished packing, she hesitated. She seemed for a moment undecided whether to take her things and leave. She stood looking at Regina Stalauskaitė, who smiled knowingly.

So my mother turned to Liuda and, in her gentle, slow and most persuasive voice, said to her, 'Liuda, think carefully before doing anything this serious. You have neither mother nor brother to advise you. You have to look to your own future. Forgive me for intruding into your personal affairs, but I think you're making a mistake. They have lived as man and wife for eighteen years and they have not, after all, been separated. He will return to her and you will become a laughing stock. Liuda, reflect. In your mother's name, I ask that you reflect before taking this step.'

A few seconds later, she added, 'Don't, Liuda, don't go through with this.'

But Liuda's eyes were consumed with a new fire, her breast rose and fell with each breath. She was very beautiful at this moment, graceful and lithe. Without a word, she picked up her things and walked out of the yurt. At the time our night shift began, the wedding in the store was going full blast. Whenever Liuda appeared outside, she'd be white as a sheet. She would retch so violently that it was painful to watch. But she'd go back in and, apparently, drink some more, then retch again. There were some who envied her, thinking she was going to be happy.

By one o'clock in the morning, all the men were drunk. Kespaiko had not invited any Lithuanians to the feast.

Just before our lunch break, at about two in the morning, Kespaiko walked over to the shore, where we were working on some rotting and foul-smelling fish. We were up to our ankles in mud, blood, salt and fish scales. Our aching hands, which had been soaking in brine all day, burned from the salt.

With our sleeves rolled up to our elbows, Marytė and I were digging in a huge vat for entrails and offal, which we dropped into buckets, to be carried to the river and dumped. It was disgusting work. The entrails stretched as they were lifted out. We would be nauseated each time we sank our hands into the vat. We would gag and then throw up. Still, it was better than sinking ulcerated hands – already raw from the salt – into brine. That's real suffering. I'd sooner get birched fifty times than soak my wounds in salt.

Kespaiko stood watching us for a long time.

'What a waste of youth.'

Then, as though he'd just remembered something, he added, 'Today is my birthday. I'm thirty-eight. Fate, eh! Will you be having lunch soon?'

'Yes.'

Then he left. The guts slipped out of my hands. I understood everything. Yesterday, I had gone to the store to buy some flour. I had a right to four kilos.

'Got any flour?' I had asked.

'How much do you want?'

'Whatever I have owing…'

'You can take as much as you like,' he said, and weighed out ten kilos. 'How about some chocolate?'

I took the chocolate. Still standing there, Kespaiko suggested I take some more food: 'Dalia, have some rice.'

'I'm out of ration cards.'

'Who cares, take the whole bag.'

'But I won't even be able to carry it.'

'Take it. I'll help you carry it.'

Thank God, I didn't get greedy and turned down the rice, but I still walked away with tinned chocolate and powdered milk. I left with a heavy heart, feeling that something bad was afoot. Regina brought home a stack of vouchers and a brand-new suit of padded trousers and jacket.

When Kespaiko asked me what time we'd be eating, it all became clear. After everyone left, I hid between the barrels and focused on the door of the store. I was not mistaken. Out came Kespaiko and Mikhail, guns slung across their shoulders. They were heading in my direction. They'd shoot me if they saw me. Suddenly, I heard rustling. I had thought I was alone. But here was Nina crouching behind me. Our eyes met. We understood each other. We'd look but not see – it was time for restraint.

Kespaiko walked up to the storage tent. He pulled out a dagger, raised it in the air and hesitated. But only for a moment. Then he slashed it open, exposing the entire stock of goods.

'There's no turning back now.' The wind carried Kespaiko's pained voice in our direction.

One after another, white sacks of flour and barley flew into the boat. Vincė was in her small tent, eating for two. I saw her poke her head out and begin counting sacks. Twelve sacks of flour, ten of barley, six of sugar, three casks of butter, two boxes of spirits. And tobacco, matches, axes, saws, nails, clothing, bedding, guns and ammunition.

The lunch break was over. I left my hiding place.

Kespaiko smiled. 'Need help?'

'I can manage.'

'You can join us, you know.'

'I don't think so.'

'Your friend Liuda will get to Lithuania before you do.'

A crowd began to gather. Kespaiko turned his gun on them: 'One more step and…'

I was afraid, for I'd overheard their conversation.

'So who's going?'

'Whoever we take along.'

That meant Kespaiko was hand-picking the ones he'd be sending to sea at night...

The three packed boats bobbed quietly in the water. All four men emerged from the store wearing brand-new padded jackets, padded trousers and boots. They were tearing woollen dresses into strips of cloth for use as shawls and foot-wraps. All of them were smashed.

Mikhail bowed to the spectators: '*Milosti proshu, magazin otkryt, berite, chto komu zablagorassuditsya.*' – 'You're welcome to take whatever you like, the store is open for business.'

Another second and the boats pushed off with their sails raised.

'Dalia, pray for me!' Liuda shouted from the boat.

Through the open window in the store, we could hear her favourite waltz still playing on the gramophone. Liuda had taken off on her ghastly honeymoon to the tune of 'I Love the Sea'. It was three o'clock in the morning. The sun was shining. For a while, the heavily laden convoy of boats was caught in a whirlpool. Eventually, a breeze picked up, the waves rose higher, the sails filled with wind and the band of daredevils, so determined to escape to America, were slowly swallowed from view by the immensity of the Arctic waters.

*

A boat left immediately for Trofimovsk. Zigmas Steponavičius and Lazauskas volunteered for the mission, as no
one else knew the way. How disgraceful that it should
have been the Lithuanians, whom Kespaiko had liked so
much, who offered to inform on him. Not that Sashka
Ivanov trusted them completely. He probably suspected
that they would stop somewhere along the way, so he
joined the two men to keep them on course. He was
candid with Grunia, saying 'The Lithuanians know everything.' Yet he had a gun too; he could have shot them.
And Mikhail wouldn't have fled, but he was afraid for
himself.

The boat sailed off. The door and window of the store
were nailed shut and the stockroom tent was repaired with
needle and thread. We were very anxious as we waited
for the NKVD, the supervisors and all the other bastards
to arrive. Everyone was fearful. In one way or another,
we had all assisted Kespaiko. It turned out that even the
bookkeeper knew he was leaving, since Kespaiko had told
her; he didn't want to get her into trouble. Apparently,
he had taken some money without authorization. Before
escaping, he signed everything that needed signing. Ivanov
also knew, as did Nina, who had been crouching behind
the casks with me. Others as well. The only one in the
dark was Grunia, poor thing. Apparently, Mikhail had
invited her along, but she thought that he was going on
an expedition, so she turned him down.

'I can't, Misha, I haven't salted the fish yet.'

'What fish? There's no fish. You should be saying "crap".

I haven't salted the "crap" yet.' Mikhail Butakov ended the conversation.

He'd been flirting seriously with Grunia and had apparently wanted to take her with him rather than Vera Chorinova – the daughter of a Yakut and a Russian woman. Like all the mixed-race women, she was attractive but had TB. She frequently bled from the mouth. Her days were probably numbered. It was just as well that they had left Grunia behind, if indeed they had been planning an escape across the sea to America.

Liuda had been persuaded into thinking that she would reach America. I had heard Regina whispering to her in the night: 'Liuda, when you get to Marijampolė, tell them where I am. Everybody knows us in Marijampolė.'

'I will, I will,' Liuda reassured Regina in a whisper.

Regina sewed the extra ration cards, for which she would be getting a lot of extra goods, into her clothes, and waited with trepidation for the cutter to arrive from Trofimovsk. I was also nervous and tried not to think about the arrival of the authorities. But fear didn't stop me or Rimantas from helping ourselves to a pile of American tinned meats and the end of a dry sausage.

A voice breaks into my sleep: 'The cutter's here. Jankovski and the police…'

I'm instantly alert, my heart pounding, and everyone is up. I'm on the shore in two minutes. The authorities are alighting from the cutter. They're all here! People from the 'fish factory', the cooperative, the Party, the police. Their rifles stand propped against each other on the deck. The helmsman is spitting into his palm and describing how they kept their guns primed and searched the horizon with binoculars. They must have thought Kespaiko would be expecting this encounter. We learned the reason for Kespaiko's escape. The last time he was in Trofimovsk, he was arrested for embezzling: the bookkeeping for the cooperative showed a shortfall of 30,000 rubles. The goods had been inventoried and confiscated. He was released by his own signature. It must have been on his return trip to Bobrovsk that he hatched his escape plan. He didn't want to go to jail, so he talked Mikhail and the girls into joining him and took off. When they unsealed the store, they were shocked by the sight. The cash register was empty. Some 50,000 rubles were missing, as were 150,000 rubles' worth of merchandise. There were empty bottles of spirits everywhere, some of them deliberately smashed. Only one unopened half-litre bottle stood on the empty shelf, a lone witness to the wretched scene.

The commission wasted no time confiscating the remaining bottle of alcohol – on Kespaiko's account. Rumour had it that they found Kespaiko's letter explaining the reason for his escape as well as a letter to his wife, Vera Pavlovna. But Jankovski took possession of all the documents and no one has seen them since. Zigmas said that when he informed Vera Pavlovna of her husband's escape, she fainted. When she regained consciousness, her first words were, 'Poor Erhard.' Even though he'd taken off with a Lithuanian girl.

Vera said that the last time he sailed for Bobrovsk, they stood on the shore for a long time saying goodbye. She said that Erhard had kissed her as though they were parting for ever. And that after he climbed into the boat, he climbed out again, kissed her hand and said, 'Vera Pavlovna, we have lived together for eighteen years... Forgive me... Forgive me...'

She had stood there mystified but with a strong sense of foreboding. Then he quickly sailed off.

She was immediately fired from her job. All those who had only yesterday smiled ingratiatingly at her, played up to her and fawned on her now grew distant and either ignored her or turned viciously against her. Even those whom she and Kespaiko had saved from starving to death by giving them bread – even they turned their backs on her.

The first person the authorities picked up was Kespaiko's fifteen-year-old niece. During her five-hour interrogation, she merely repeated, 'I don't know, I didn't know, I've never received anything from him.'

In fact, he had given her 30,000 rubles, but she alone knew where the money was hidden.

My own fear turned out to be baseless – no one interrogated me. Gradually, everything returned to normal. The store reopened for business. The authorities left.

The monotonous days returned, as did the downpours. Each day we arrived home drenched from our twelve-hour shifts in the rain. Our clothes turned white with the salt and stiff as armour. They reeked of fish. In the evenings, when we laid our padded trousers and jackets out to dry inside the yurt – clothes that were slimy with the blood, salt and entrails of rotting fish – the stench was beyond nauseating.

The odour of an outhouse is actually easier to take. Frequently, when we hung up our smelly work clothes, underwear and foot-wraps in the evenings, we gagged and retched. And now we were knee-deep in our yurt as well. The roof could not hold back a driving rain, so we were soaked in water all day – outside at work and inside at home. Yet no one came down with tonsillitis or flu. Before this, I used to have chronic tonsillitis, but I've felt no sign of it here.

We work pretty much without supervision. Grunia can't watch us twenty-four hours a day. We've been robbing the place blind.

Since the beginning of summer, the two barrels used to salt the fish continue to remain only half full. We can't seem to fill them to the brim. According to the records and invoices, the fishermen have brought in close to five tonnes of fish. But whenever there is no fresh catch, we steal the fish we salted yesterday right out of the barrel. We soak it briefly in water and eat it. Every day, Grunia stands watch over the barrels, waiting until we leave to secure the lids with huge rocks, but we watch for an opportune moment, roll off the rocks and... well, the fish keep disappearing. There are times when I scare myself just thinking how appalling this passion of ours has become. Stealing has become our daily bread. There was an empty yurt nearby. Our supervisors pleaded with us not to touch it; they even threatened us. But five days later not a sign of it was left – it had gone up in flames in our stove. The only thing remaining of the large yurt we had burned for firewood was a pile of sod.

We've all equipped ourselves with knives, axes, shovels, saws and enough salt and fat reserves to last us a year. We even filled our cans with kerosene oil to get us through the long polar nights.

The first yurt is occupied by two tramps, Vorobyova and Yudina, creatures of indeterminate age and gender and unbelievably ragged. Gorky's 'barefoot' poor look like English lords by comparison. Vorobyova wears enormous army boots that have no soles and hardly any uppers. She wears her foot-wraps unravelled, dragging half a metre of cloth behind her through the mud. Her padded trousers and jacket are worn against bare skin. The cotton batting is coming out in tufts and her unwashed body is visible through the tears in the fabric. The headgear of this twenty-three-year-old (according to her documents) has ear flaps that hang down to her knees, so they trail behind her like wings when she walks, though their colour and fabric are no longer recognizable. She sleeps on bare planks and for months on end removes neither her shoes nor her clothes. She comes to work as the spirit moves her, usually after a good night's sleep – at ten or so. When our arms are ready to give out and have begun to ache from carrying fish on stretchers all morning, the figure of Vorobyova appears on the horizon. She walks slowly, her hands in her pockets, and approaches the salting station without paying the least attention to our teasing or our jokes.

'*Lidia Vasilyevna, kak vashe samochuvstviye?*' – 'How are we this morning? Have we slept well?' someone asks ironically, addressing her by her first name and patronymic. The audience falls silent: a performance is about to begin.

Lidia stops. Then, without moving a centimetre and keeping her hands in her pockets, she slowly turns her head in the direction of the voice. With the haughty squint of a duchess, she gives the owner of the voice a once-over, while she decides whether to dignify the sarcasm with a reply.

Deciding in the affirmative, she answers disdainfully – mispronouncing the '*kh*', '*Nichego, khorosho.*' – 'Fine, can't complain.'

We dissolve into laughter. But Vorobyova is unflappable. Not a muscle in her face twitches. Which makes us howl even louder. We laugh till our sides split. Vorobyova stands there motionless, she doesn't even blink. By now, we're hysterical. If she had just chuckled, I don't think she would have been at all funny, but her composure cracks us up every time. We lose control. I wonder if anyone can be more laid-back than Lidia. She doesn't get worked up about anything. Kespaiko, who wanted to force her to exert herself, confiscated her bread-ration card. She didn't become any more industrious. She just took to eating raw fish, because she was too lazy to cook it. When she got diarrhoea, she spent hours squatting outside Kespaiko's house – her rump facing his window.

The winner in this siege was always Lidia Vasilyevna Vorobyova. Eventually, Kespaiko gave up and handed back her ration card. The problem is that a person like that fears nothing. The authorities have no ace that they can play against her. She pilfered fish openly, even when the supervisor was standing right next to her. She'd take her time at the trough, inspecting the fish as if she owned it, just trying to identify a good one. When she found what she liked, she hooked her fingers under its gills and carried it home.

'Stealing?' Kespaiko once asked her, thinking that his stern tone would have the desired effect.

She stopped, assessed him with her usual look and replied, 'Borrowing.' Then strode home to dinner. She's not afraid of prison and she isn't a fighter; prison would suit her fine. The supervisors, seeing that she looked almost indecently naked, drew on government funds to get her some clothes. She would never buy them herself because she doesn't have the money and, in any case, she doesn't care. I don't make fun of her, so, occasionally, she talks to me. But all I've learned about her is that at one time she was a nurse. Then the politics of the period seduced her into going north. Someone who had travelled with her on the first convoy said that she'd been nicely dressed, that she had a watch, a change of underwear, that she was being accompanied by a mother who wept during the journey. En route, Lidia sold off her things for practically nothing. Lots of people took advantage of her – borrowed her things without returning them. Still, how could someone become so slovenly? What could make someone revert to such a primal state?

I felt sorry for her when Kespaiko harassed her because, in spite of everything, she still had her pride. After all, she's human too and has a mother who would probably give anything to see her. How painful it would be to see her daughter a laughing stock. Lidia hated Kespaiko. While he was packing things in preparation for his escape, she watched him in her usual unruffled manner, with her hands in her pockets and a bland smile on her face. Then she said, her voice resonating in the silence, '*Modestovich, provalivay na* —' – 'Modestovich, get the — out...'

The uncensored expletive was her only rebuttal to his taunting. I like Vorobyova, I like her pride. I admire the fact that she still feels like a human being, still feels that she has value as a person. Perhaps she senses my admiration. She doesn't avoid me; in fact, she's become quite attached. We often supply her with flour. Once Lidia and I found ourselves alone together. It was a lunch break. Grunia was busy registering the incoming fish. Everyone was swiping, snaffling, stealing whatever came to hand. I grabbed some lard and prepared to sneak home with it. But the magnitude of what I saw next stopped me in my tracks. Lidia pulled out a knife used to gut fish – she'd stolen that too – and with a grand swing of her arm sheared off nearly the whole side of the storage tent.

'I need foot-wraps,' she explained, and slipped a huge section of the tent into her trousers.

We sped home so fast we could have broken the record for the 500-metre dash. I could hardly hang on to my booty for laughing so hard. Boy, did we have a long way to go towards achieving socialism. After lunch there was trouble. Grunia, Nina, who is technically the watchman though the only watching she ever did was on pay day, Sonia the bookkeeper and the workers all rushed to the scene. Everyone was furious, aghast. They couldn't imagine who the culprit might be. The unflappable Vorobyova was the only one there who remained calm, above it all, looking down from some transcendent height at people making a commotion over something she considered trivial. The tent had indeed been ruined. She'd sliced right through the two American sacks from which it had been sewn. Taking the tent down and repairing it will cost twenty times more than it did to put it up. I told Lidia as much.

She looked at me as if I had lost my mind and said, '*U gosudarstva karman shiroky, ne bespokoysya.*' – 'The state's pockets are deep, don't worry about it.'

In time, I came to realize that this was the thinking of most Soviet citizens. The only difference between them was how and what they took. But everyone pilfered, stole, helped themselves to whatever they could get their hands on.

The other one was Yulia Ivanovna Yudina. She was here by mistake. She'd been swept up together with the Finns during the evacuation of Leningrad. It is hard to guess her age; she claims to be twenty-three. Yulia is a talker and an incredible thief, but she steals in secret. Being a couple of proud women, both Lidia and Yulia steal only from the state; they haven't taken a thing from us. The Finns said that Yulia's father had been a navy captain in Leningrad. She's smart and witty. I once asked her why everyone stole so much. She replied, 'With us, theft is a matter of honour and proof of courage.' And then added, 'And necessity, if you don't want to starve like a dog.' She had a point. Yulia's toilette differed little from Lidia's. It was hard to call her padded jacket 'padded'. As for her bottom half – beyond words. Seeing her naked like that, Mavrin ordered that she be given three metres of cloth. She took the cloth, but didn't make herself any clothes. She just folded it, wrapped it around her bottom half and tied the two corners into a knot. And that's how she walks about in public. When she's in a rush and limping, because one of her feet suffered frostbite this winter, the cloth parts at the side and billows like a flag. At night, she unwraps herself and uses it as a blanket. Yulia would be a real beauty if she weren't such a slob. Her large black eyes, black hair and attractive figure turn heads even in her current condition.

A Yakut returning from a hunting trip told us that on one of the Lena islands not far from the sea he had come across an empty butter cask with a card inside that read: 'E. M. Kespaiko sailed through here on 8 August at 3 o'clock in the afternoon.'

I visited a Yakut yurt. It houses about forty people and is horribly dank. Yakuts are all tubercular – 98 per cent of the population, according to medical experts. Oddly enough, the city of Yakutsk has a dry climate, yet the mortality there of people with TB is very high. But here it's damp, cold and rainy, with permafrost. Summer and winter, the yurts sit on icy tundra. In other words, this place has a typically humid seaside climate. Yet TB sufferers in Bobrovsk find their condition easier to bear. Most of the Yakuts here are also starving, because the fishing is poor and not all of them can hunt, so they work at the factory salting fish. They cough up blood everywhere and some of it, naturally, lands on the fish, but no one cares. We won't be the ones eating it! The Yakuts have all been baptized at some point by Russian patriarchs and adopted their surnames – Belousov, Kirilov, Achasov, Sidorov, Olenikov, Pavlov. But the Orthodox faith never really took hold among them. The Yakuts continue to believe in their own gods and evil spirits. Some places still have shamans. All Yakuts smoke pipes – men, women, old people and children. Even nursing infants reach for their mothers' pipes and inhale the potent smoke. All the children have rickets: the reason Yakuts are bow-legged. Their men are short, with concave chests, their hair coal-black and coarse. As with other Oriental races, the men are beardless. One of them, Gogolev, has some growth on his chin – a sparse grey beard like that of a billy goat. The mortality rate is very high, especially among children. Trachoma is a fact of life. The Yakuts work on the fish with red, runny eyes, inevitably infecting it with TB and trachoma germs. A lot of us have already picked up scabies from them. We share the same knives to gut fish, the same stretchers to carry the fish from the tables where they're washed to the ones where they're salted. Entering a Yakut dugout deep underground is like entering an ancient Greek *prytaneum* – but in Shanghai. It is filled with smoke from the hearth in the centre of the room. The Yakuts drink strong tea, smoke opium, which they obtain from who knows where, and gamble at cards. Naked children with distended bellies and bandy legs roll on the floor. The Yakuts love their children and display a strong sense of solidarity. If the supervisor is a Yakut, he will hire his own people. A dying race needs to be unified. Besides, they are also a proud people, so when they get angry or have been drinking the knives come out.

They hate the Russians and aren't particularly sympathetic to Lithuanians, but knowing that we weren't brought to Yakutia voluntarily, they try to be tolerant. The Yakuts in Bobrovsk originally came from Yakutsk, so they've seen something of the wider world. They call all white people *nenchia* – meaning 'owls', because our eyes are large. Consequently, they find us unattractive. Among Yakuts, a mere slit for an eye is considered a mark of beauty. Frequently, whenever a Yakut woman gets upset with one of us and wishes to insult her, she will make circles with her fingers and say, '*Kusichan karaulan.*' – 'Big, ugly eyes.' We find that amusing and we laugh.

A cutter arrives. A new supervisor has come to Bobrovsk, the Yakut Makarov. He swears at everyone and praises himself: 100 per cent Asian. He orders everyone processing fish in Bobrovsk to move to Tumat. Mum has been sick, the trip is by open boat and there's a storm in progress. I go to Makarov to ask whether he'd let us stay in Bobrovsk. He listens and then, looking me in the eye, asks, like someone who thinks I've just betrayed my country, 'I take it the front line is important to you? And you have to work, don't you? So what are you talking about? What mother? You'll be a mother yourself soon!'

I look at him – a psychopath. I return to the yurt and do not leave for Tumat. Makarov doesn't notice our absence in the large crowd of people; he's too busy shouting, scolding and threatening everyone with arrest. From a distance, I watch people boarding boats. The last to arrive are Vorobyova and Yudina. They're in no hurry; they move with the gravity of people contemplating matters of state.

The helmsman and other men greet them with a wave of laughter: '*Ey, Vorobyova, chemodan pogruzila? Ey, gde tvoy bagazh?*' – 'Hey, Vorobyova, have you brought your suitcase? Hey, where's your luggage?'

She stands there like a newborn – without a pot, spoon or hat to her name. She owns nothing except what she's got to cover her body. Whatever luggage she has, she's wearing.

The Sirutis family – Marytė, who is my age, and her mother – also stay behind, as do Balčiuvienė and Dovydaitienė with their children, and also Steponavičienė. There is no more work to be done at the salting stations. The commission has certified that the fish is substandard. Everything the fishermen caught – all that effort – is dumped in the river. All 500 barrels. We froze, our hands bled, they developed sores, the salt ate away at our skin, the work was hard – all for nothing. And that's not even counting the expense to the state. The disgusting stench from the shore has spread over the whole of Bobrovsk. Even the starving dogs give us a wide berth, keeping a whole kilometre between themselves and our factory.

Mavrin put the blame for the spoiled fish entirely on Kespaiko and was glad to hand over whatever was left of the enterprise to Makarov. Even though that's hugely unfair of Mavrin, it's neither here nor there to Kespaiko now. Ten allegations, or eleven – what difference does it make?

We are back to gathering firewood from the surrounding islands. Each day we are transported by rowing boat across one of the channels to an island. On a three-kilometre walk along the shore, we find lots of driftwood, including different-sized logs. These we will stack for the winter, at which point they will be brought to Bobrovsk by dog sledge or by us. They will be used to heat the store and the office. We're a crew of eight women – four Lithuanians and four Finns. The Finns work non-stop and are very scrupulous about stacking the wood compactly so as not to leave the centre of the stack empty. Working in their brigade means working just like them. But then at night, back in Bobrovsk, Marytė and I can barely move. Our insides ache from the strain of lifting wood to the top of the stacks. The pain in Marytė's lower abdomen is excruciating. Last year, she ruptured something while lifting sacks. We're just not physically mature enough for this kind of work. We lose our appetite, we feel nauseous, we drop onto our pallets as soon as we get home. But what to do? I begin to hatch a plan. Life and hard work force my hand.

The following day, I suggest to Marytė that the two of us work apart from the Finns.

'Let's do that,' agrees Marytė.

The Finns find a site that has more driftwood and begin to work like tractors.

'Marytė, I want you to hear me out. Let me be team leader. I'll present our work for inspection and I'll decide when to work and when to rest. If you want to work with me and not with the others, then humour me and follow my lead.'

Marytė agrees. I explain to her that there's no point in working hard, that we will not get rich doing it but merely hunchbacked, that there's no reason to be scrupulously honest either, that we're not obliged to sacrifice our adolescent health to the state, that we're going to need it ourselves, and that the state has already taken everything else we had. It has robbed us of our homeland and our parents and our homes and our childhoods; it has turned us into slaves and our lives into shit. So... if we have to work, let it be with our heads, not our hands. Marytė stared at me in amazement, obviously thunderstruck by my modern ideas. At one point, I almost had her in tears.

We begin to work. In no time at all, we stack a pile of wood about two metres square in size – with a hollow centre big enough to hold three people. And sturdy enough, I hope, not to collapse before we get home. Our abdomens are feeling fine. Then we rest for several hours. I tell Marytė about the theatre, the opera, we sing arias, we cry our hearts out talking about our school days and the shows. Afterwards, we stretch out on the logs for a nap. Towards evening, we stack another pile, this one four metres square in size. Grunia arrives to check off our work. I tell Marytė to keep a straight face. I present our hollow stacks for inspection – Grunia notices nothing out of the ordinary. Then I show her the stack six metres square that the Finns built yesterday and which Grunia has already inspected. But she doesn't remember that because she's much too distracted. She spends her nights singing romantic ballads with the radio men. So she checks this one off as well. She measures it herself, she doesn't trust me. But wanting to prove to her how conscientious I am, I keep telling her, 'No, Grunia, you've added three additional centimetres. That's not right! I want to receive only what I've earned.'

Touched by the purity of my heart, she tells me to multiply the width, length and height because she does not know how to do it herself. So I do the multiplication for her and add a few centimetres for good measure.

'You must be tired, girls. You've done a lot today…'

Marytė flutters her long, lovely lashes and mumbles, 'It was hard, Grunia, you can imagine. They were such big logs.'

That day we return home not a bit tired. After dinner, we sit a long time on the doorstep, singing one of my favourite songs:

> We sing as we march,
> Our youth leads the way,

All the fields resound,
With a wonderful sound.

Sing on, happy youth,
Sing on, sing on.
The past can't return,
That we must learn.

The next day Marytė would not have left my side for all the cake in the world. That's the way we worked the whole time. We'd resubmit yesterday's stacks and find a variety of ways to fool the naive Grunia. Well, not her personally, but the state. Soon those stacks would be covered with snow. Everyone who wasn't too lazy would be hauling them in. No one was going to remember how many stacks there were in all. For the first time since we had been deported, we enjoyed something of a holiday. We worked little and felt no hunger. Marytė recovered her health and perked up. She's a pretty girl. Tall. Looks eighteen, though she's only fifteen. Zigmas melts at the sight of her. The last lingering days of the polar summer are slipping away. Some of the days are beautiful. There are even two days during which we can shed our padded jackets. The waters encircling us are still as mirrors with a hint of warmth. But not for long. The wind off the sea picks up again, the waters turn black and waves pound the shore… Our small yurt stands right near the water. The foaming surf rolls practically up to our doorstep. The sound of the sea lulls us to sleep; the sound of the sea wakes us up. Not for a minute does it let us forget where we are. Lithuania seems like a dream, a mirage. When we talk about her, we can hardly believe that there is such a country and that we once lived there. A cold autumn arrives on the shores of the Arctic Ocean. The final days of navigation are upon us. It is the end of October. A thin ten-centimetre layer of snow, which had covered the tundra like a tunic and had begun to melt in the warmth of the sun, has turned to ice again. We are waiting for the barge to arrive with the entire Lithuanian fishermen's cooperative. Winter fishing is about to begin.

Two radio men arrive. Muscular, handsome men from Leningrad, who have been knocking about the North since 1937. Most recently, they were radio operators at the harbour in Tiksi. Here they erect a radio tower and set up a temporary radio station in a tent. They invite Marytė and me to come and listen to the radio. One evening after work, we cross their threshold. The first thing that stuns us is the electric light bulb – they have a generator. The sight of it takes our breath away. We restrain our amazement when we notice the radio men smiling at us. They stand there politely, pretending not to notice, but they understand everything perfectly. They invite us to sit down. The news report on the battles in Stalingrad is about to end, the time is announced. Eager to please us, the radio men search the stations for music. We hear voices in French, then English, and suddenly, the most enchanting music. *Swan Lake*. No, not in a dream. Real music, music… music… It is our life, our childhood, our home, our parents, school – like a bolt of lightning, the past flashes before our eyes. Lithuania, that far-off country, the land of our dreams, is in the room with us. I don't know exactly what happened next. I just remember jumping up and running onto the tundra, falling face down in the snow and crying. Rivers of tears until we could hardly breathe for the tightness in our throats. I have no idea how long we lay there trembling – the frozen tundra in our embrace – and sobbing. Our stolen youth weeping for its stolen homeland.

But nothing stays for ever and our anguish passed. Pale and shivering from the cold and the shock, we returned to our small yurt. A piercing wind was blowing in from the sea and the waves were crashing madly against the shore, spraying us with salt water.

Afterword

The twentieth century is with good reason called the century of the concentration camp or of deportation. In this period Central and Eastern Europe experienced two totalitarian dictatorships, one under Hitler and one under Stalin. Both were intent on crushing for ever the free spirit of the individual; both created systems of terror and death from which there was to be no way out. But through great endeavour and sacrifice a way out was found, and today Lithuania is part of the democratic world. What occurred in the era of these two dictatorships represents perhaps the most vital of human experiences. No testimony from this time must ever be forgotten.

Relatively few testimonies remain of the Stalinist Gulag system – which incidentally outlived Stalin. Soviet censorship sought to efface testimonies, and laid a veil of lies and dissimulation over this period. Such attempts, moreover, did not cease after the collapse of the USSR. In many cases political prisoners and exiles – if they were still alive – did not dare talk about their experiences. Some never believed that their accounts would find an audience and others felt that their suffering was inexpressible in

Dalia at a reunion with fellow deportees in Kaunas, 1958.

words, that it was at the very limit of human language. Despite this, the silence was broken. Important accounts of the Gulag do exist, most notably those of Alexander Solzhenitsyn and Varlam Shalamov, among others. They made a significant contribution to the dissolution of the Soviet totalitarian system. I am convinced that the testimony of the Lithuanian Dalia Grinkevičiūtė ranks alongside these famous works.

Dalia shared the fate of many of her fellow Lithuanians. In 1940 her homeland, a small country on the Baltic Sea where people lived a modest but comparatively peaceful and civilized existence, was occupied by Stalin's army. One year later, just before the beginning of the German–Soviet war, virtually the entire political, economic and cultural elite of Lithuania – irrespective of their background, nationality or beliefs – were plucked from their surroundings and very quickly resettled in the far eastern regions of the USSR, thousands of kilometres from home. The exiles were strictly guarded as they were transported in cattle wagons, and many died en route, the first to perish being the elderly, women and children. The inhabitants of Latvia, Estonia, western Ukraine and western Belarus suffered the same fate.

Dalia, a fourteen-year-old girl at the time, ended up in the most perilous area for exiles: by the Laptev Sea in the Arctic Ocean, where the climate and living conditions were similar to northern Greenland or worse. Many of Dalia's fellow exiles died in this icy hell – from cold, starvation or disease. Dalia, however, did not give up; not only did she survive, she also succeeded in escaping. She was rearrested, interned in a camp and sent into exile again. After Stalin's death she managed to return to Lithuania.

When Dalia finished her medical studies she worked as a doctor in a provincial town. She continued to suffer persecution and harassment from the regime, but won the trust and love of the local population. They called her 'Daktarė Dalytė' (Dr Dalietta): the use of pet names in Lithuanian suggests deep affection and warm relationships.

She died in 1987 at the age of 60, leaving behind one of the most important and harrowing testimonies of life in a Gulag.

TOMAS VENCLOVA
Lithuanian poet, essayist and professor of literature, USA, 2018

Subscribe

Discover the best of contemporary European literature: subscribe to Peirene Press and receive a world-class novella from us three times a year, direct to your door. The books are sent out six weeks before they are available in bookshops and online.

Your subscription will allow us to plan ahead with confidence and help us to continue to introduce English readers to the joy of new foreign literature for many years to come.

> *'A class act.'* GUARDIAN

> *'Two-hour books to be devoured in a single sitting: literary cinema for those fatigued by film.'*
> TIMES LITERARY SUPPLEMENT

A one year subscription costs £35 (3 books, free p&p for UK)

Please sign up via our online shop at www.peirenepress.com/shop

BASMEH & ZEITOONEH
RELIEF & DEVELOPMENT

Peirene is proud to support Basmeh & Zeitooneh.

Basmeh & Zeitooneh (The Smile & The Olive) is
a Lebanese-registered NGO. It was established in
2012 in response to the Syrian refugee crisis.
B&Z aims to create opportunities for refugees to
move beyond being victims of conflict and help
them to become empowered individuals who one
day will return to their own country to rebuild
their society. Today the organization is managing
nine community centres in the region: seven in
Lebanon and two in Turkey.

Peirene will donate 50p from the sale of this book
to the charity. Thank you for buying this book.

www.basmeh-zeitooneh.org